John Steinbeck's
THE
GRAPES OF WRATH

Bloom's
NOTES

Edited and with an Introduction by
HAROLD BLOOM

First Printing
1 3 5 7 9 8 6 4 2

ISBN 0-7910-3685-5

Chelsea House Publishers
1974 Sproul Road, Suite 400
P.O. Box 914
Broomall, PA 19008-0914

Contents

User's Guide   4

Introduction   5

Biography of John Steinbeck   8

Thematic and Structural Analysis   12

List of Characters   24

Critical Views   27

Books by John Steinbeck   64

Works about John Steinbeck and *The Grapes of Wrath*   67

Index of Themes and Ideas   71

User's Guide

This volume is designed to present biographical, critical, and bibliographical information on John Steinbeck and *The Grapes of Wrath.* Following Harold Bloom's introduction, there appears a detailed biography of the author, discussing the major events in his life and his important literary works. Then follows a thematic and structural analysis of the work, in which significant themes, patterns, and motifs are traced. An annotated list of characters supplies brief information on the chief characters in the work.

A selection of critical extracts, derived from previously published material by leading critics, then follows. The extracts consist of statements by the author on his work, early reviews of the work, and later evaluations down to the present day. The items are arranged chronologically by date of first publication. A bibliography of Steinbeck's writings (including a complete listing of all books he wrote, cowrote, edited, and translated in his lifetime, and important posthumous publications), a list of additional books and articles on him and on *The Grapes of Wrath,* and an index of themes conclude the volume.

Harold Bloom is Sterling Professor of the Humanities at Yale University and Henry W. and Albert A. Berg Professor of English at the New York University Graduate School. He is the author of twenty books and the editor of more than thirty anthologies of literature and literary criticism.

Professor Bloom's works include *Shelley's Mythmaking* (1959), *The Visionary Company* (1961), *Blake's Apocalypse* (1963), *Yeats* (1970), *A Map of Misreading* (1975), *Kabbalah and Criticism* (1975), and *Agon: Towards a Theory of Revisionism* (1982). *The Anxiety of Influence* (1973) sets forth Professor Bloom's provocative theory of the literary relationships between the great writers and their predecessors. His most recent books are *The American Religion* (1992) and *The Western Canon* (1994).

Professor Bloom earned his Ph.D. from Yale University in 1955 and has served on the Yale faculty since then. He is a 1985 MacArthur Foundation Award recipient and served as the Charles Eliot Norton Professor of Poetry at Harvard University in 1987–88. He is currently the editor of the Chelsea House series Major Literary Characters and Modern Critical Views, and other Chelsea House series in literary criti-

Introduction

HAROLD BLOOM

The Grapes of Wrath is a flawed but permanent American book, and its continued popularity, after well more than half a century, seems to indicate that it is anything but a period-piece. In the age of Gingrich and his allies, the Christian Right, Steinbeck's prose epic has a fresh capacity to offend our pillars of society. Steinbeck's Okies are detached by him from traditional Protestantism and believe instead in a curious but very American religion of their own, in which the lapsed minister Jim Casy is a secular Jesus Christ and his survivor, Tom Joad, is a kind of St. Paul of social rebellion. Though Steinbeck's prose is perpetually imbued with the King James Bible (and Hemingway), Casy's own Bible reduces to a single book, Ecclesiastes or the Preacher, the most skeptical writing that is canonized as part of the Hebrew Bible or Christian Old Testament. Casy's radical and naturalistic humanism has clear sources in Ralph Waldo Emerson's vision of the Oversoul and in Walt Whitman's love of the democratic masses, yet its darker overtones derive from the tragic Preacher of Ecclesiastes. When Jim Casy declares the holiness of human sexuality or of breakfast, he does not rely upon God as his authority, and Tom Joad does not become an outcast prophet in the name of a Lord who is trampling out the vintage where the grapes of wrath are stored. Tom Joad, American in his self-reliance, will stamp them out for himself, and for those dispossessed with him.

As an American epic, *The Grapes of Wrath* never loses its polemical edge, which is populist rather than Marxist. The English novelist Anthony Burgess, who recognized shrewdly that Hemingway was Steinbeck's trouble, noted also that Steinbeck was precisely what he asserted himself to be, a Jeffersonian Democrat. I myself tend to think of Steinbeck as the Harry Truman of American novelists: kindly, honorable, pugnacious, and opposed to all forces of exploitation. The shadow of Hemingway hovers over every descriptive passage in *The Grapes of Wrath,* yet for once the book is wholly Steinbeck's own. There is nothing of Hemingway in its stance towards America, though the prose filters the King James Bible's rhetoric through Hemingway's mode of writing about the object-world. As has been noted frequently by critics, the women of *The Grapes of Wrath* are stronger than the men, except for the prophets Jim Casy and Tom Joad, and yet they are not the devouring women of Hemingway and of Scott Fitzgerald. The endurance of Ma Joad and of Rose of Sharon is one of the ornaments of *The Grapes of Wrath.*

Why should the best of Steinbeck's women seem less overdetermined than the men, or quite simply, why does Ma Joad have more freedom of the will than her son Tom does? Why are Steinbeck's men more of a social group, their fates settled by economics, when his outstanding women are able to manifest an acute individuality? Is Ma Joad's passion for keeping her hard-pressed family together merely an instinctual reflex? Certainly, without her will and drive, Tom Joad would not have had the desire to carry on for the martyred Jim Casy. One could argue that *The Grapes of Wrath* weakens as it approaches its conclusion, and that only Ma Joad keeps this trailing-off from becoming an aesthetic catastrophe. Confused as Steinbeck becomes, mixing allegorical and ironic elements into a previously realistic plot, the consistency of Ma Joad helps the novelist firm up an otherwise wavering structure. It is curious that rereading the novel can be a less rewarding experience than reseeing the film, where the young Henry Fonda's performance as Tom Joad compensates for some of the contradictions built into the character. The achieved pathos of Fonda's acting helps obscure Steinbeck's inability to persuade us that Tom Joad ends with a more fully articulated sense of identity than he possessed at the onset of the story.

Steinbeck's naturalistic humanism itself seems confused: do his characters fall into animal-like behavior because of society's oppressions, or because they simply revert to their true identity when they are uprooted? Morale is a category that has validity in Hemingway, where you can show courage and assert your dignity against grave odds or else collapse into a failure of nerve. Steinbeck, Hemingway's involuntary disciple, generally cannot keep so clear a vision as to whether the human will is significantly free or not. Ma Joad tells us that the people go on, despite all the injustices that they suffer; we come to believe that the Joads go on mostly because of her firm matriarchal will. Perhaps Steinbeck's true strength in this too-ambitious novel is that the spirit of Ecclesiastes is more movingly incarnated in Ma Joad than in the prophets Jim Casy and Tom Joad. She, and to a lesser extent Rose of Sharon, have the indestructible endurance that rises up from the wisdom of an ultimate skepticism, one that expects nothing and so cannot know defeat. ❖

Biography of
John Steinbeck

John Ernst Steinbeck, Jr., was born on February 27, 1902, to John Ernst and Olive Hamilton Steinbeck in Salinas, a small agricultural community in the north central part of California. He read voraciously as a youth; he was particularly fascinated by Sir Thomas Malory's *Morte d'Arthur* (c. 1470), and this retelling of the legends of King Arthur influenced him for his whole life. Steinbeck graduated from Salinas High School in 1919 and entered Stanford University the next year, taking courses in science and becoming interested in marine biology. Although he studied at Stanford intermittently for five years, he finally left without a degree.

In 1925 Steinbeck moved to New York City, where he began working for a newspaper, the New York *American.* He was a very poor reporter, however, because he would get too emotionally involved in the stories he was writing, so he returned to California by working as a deckhand on a ship. Finding a job as a caretaker in Lake Tahoe, Nevada, he devoted himself to writing and produced an adventure story about a Caribbean pirate, *Cup of Gold,* published in 1929. The next year he married Carol Henning and settled in Pacific Grove, California. At this time he formed a close friendship with noted marine biologist Edward F. Ricketts, who for many years was Steinbeck's mentor and critic. Their expedition in 1940 to the Gulf of California was the basis for *Sea of Cortez* (1941), and Ricketts appears as a character in several other works.

Steinbeck's first book went largely unnoticed, as did his next two, *The Pastures of Heaven* (1932) and *To a God Unknown* (1933), both of which are set in California. His first significant recognition came with the publication of *Tortilla Flat* (1935), a tale of Mexican-American vagabonds in the Monterey area. The $3000 Steinbeck received for the movie rights to this short novel helped to lift him out of the poverty he had experienced as a struggling writer in the Great Depression. In 1936 his novel *In Dubious Battle,* dealing with a fruit pickers' strike in California, caused considerable controversy. The next year

Steinbeck cemented his reputation with *Of Mice and Men* (1937), which remains one of the most widely read works in American literature. Steinbeck was praised for his accomplishments as a writer in the American idiom, and the play version of *Of Mice and Men* (1937), on which he worked with the famous playwright George S. Kaufman, won the New York Drama Critics' Circle Award and was made into a film starring Burgess Meredith and Lon Chaney, Jr. Steinbeck used the proceeds from the book and play to travel widely in Europe.

Returning to California, Steinbeck spent much time in the camps of migrant workers. This led directly to *The Grapes of Wrath* (1939), an epic of dispossessed Oklahoma sharecroppers in search of a promised land in California. The novel was extremely topical and also crystallized themes that remained prominent in Steinbeck's writings thereafter: concern for the working classes, the preying of men upon one another, and sentimental attachments to land and community. It was the best-selling book of 1939, won the Pulitzer Prize for fiction in 1940, and was made into an acclaimed film.

Steinbeck divorced his wife Carol in 1942 and married Gwyndolen Conger the next year; they had two sons. Much of his writing of this period focused on World War II, including *Bombs Away* (1942), a book designed to convince Americans of the importance of the air force, and *The Moon Is Down* (1942), a short novel about the German occupation of a small town in Norway. He spent the latter half of 1943 in Europe as a special correspondent for the *New York Herald Tribune,* and his reports were later collected as *Once There Was a War* (1958). Steinbeck was traumatized by the suffering he witnessed among the troops; as if to banish these memories, upon his return he wrote the novel *Cannery Row* (1945), a nostalgic look at life in Monterey before the war.

In 1945 Steinbeck settled in New York City with his wife and sons. In 1947 he published the well-known short novel *The Pearl,* an allegory based on a Mexican folk tale. A trip to Russia in 1947 led to the writing of *A Russian Journal* (1948), with photographs by Robert Capa. Although Steinbeck was elected to the American Academy of Arts and Letters, both his personal life and his literary career became troubled around this time:

he divorced his wife in 1948; his friend Ed Ricketts died in an accident; and his recent works were poorly received, especially the play *Burning Bright* (1950), which closed after only thirteen performances on Broadway. Steinbeck turned to writing screenplays, including the radical political film *Viva Zapata!* (1950), directed by Elia Kazan. In 1950 he married Elaine Scott.

While living alternately in New York and Nantucket, Steinbeck wrote *East of Eden* (1952), a long novel about a man who marries a prostitute; it partly restored his literary reputation. He and his wife spent the next several years in Europe, and Steinbeck sent reports of his travels to *Collier's* and the *Saturday Review*. He returned to the United States briefly in 1952 to work as a speechwriter for Adlai Stevenson's presidential campaign.

Steinbeck settled in Sag Harbor, Long Island, in 1955, and the next year he again assisted in Adlai Stevenson's bid for the presidency; but after Stevenson lost, Steinbeck spent much of the next three years in England studying Malory's *Morte d'Arthur*. The light-hearted political satire *The Short Reign of Pippin IV* was published in 1957. Steinbeck's final novel was *The Winter of Our Discontent* (1961), a story of life in Long Island.

Disillusioned by the failure of Adlai Stevenson's third presidential bid in 1960 (he lost the Democratic nomination to John F. Kennedy), Steinbeck set out to rediscover America, in the company of his dog Charley. The three-month trip in the latter half of 1960 led to the writing of *Travels with Charley* (1962), a work that did much to restore Steinbeck's fading reputation. In 1962 he was also awarded the Nobel Prize for literature. Steinbeck continued to spend much time traveling in Europe, although he returned to the United States in 1964 to work on Lyndon B. Johnson's presidential campaign. At this time he also received the United States Medal of Freedom. In 1965 he began writing a series of letters to Alicia Paterson Guggenheim, publisher of the Long Island newspaper *Newsday,* from various locations around the world, including Israel and Vietnam. These letters were controversial for their criticism of the increasing rebelliousness of American youth and for their support of American involvement in the Vietnam War. A later volume,

America and Americans (1966), repeats some of these criticisms but otherwise affirms Steinbeck's faith in his country's future.

John Steinbeck died in New York City on December 20, 1968. Many of his letters and uncollected essays have been published posthumously, but Steinbeck's reputation continues to rest on his searing political and social novels of the 1930s. Although scorned by some critics for being superficial and excessively moralistic, he remains one of the most popular and respected American authors of the century. ❖

Thematic and Structural Analysis

The Grapes of Wrath tells the bitter story of the Joad family as it struggles to survive and to maintain its dignity in the middle of the Great Depression. But it is also the story of a whole class of people like the Joads, tenant farmers who have lost their land and decide to move to California in hope of finding a better life. Steinbeck makes explicit his aim to write a social novel about the plight of these tenant farmers by alternating between a narrative of the Joad family and a description of the larger experience of the dispossessed as they migrate West.

The novel begins in the drought-stricken fields of Oklahoma. The sun shrivels the green crops that have been planted during the brief spring rains, and it washes the color out of the soil. Strong, steady winds blow the dirt up into the sky and cover the land, the houses, and the poor farmers hiding in them with a layer of finely powdered dust. The first ten chapters of *The Grapes of Wrath* occur in this dust bowl locale, where the harsh forces of nature test the stubborn stoicism of the men and women who scratch out a living on rented land.

Tom Joad enters this scene in **Chapter Two.** Just released from prison, where he served four years for manslaughter, Tom convinces a truck driver to give him a ride over the last bit of terrain to his home. The driver tells Tom that the company he works for has a policy against hitchhikers. But Tom replies that he was hoping the driver could prove himself a "good guy even if some rich bastard makes [him] carry a sticker" that says "NO RIDERS." The driver feels trapped by the logic of Tom's argument and allows him to climb into the cab, but only after they have pulled away from the rest stop. This confrontation foreshadows a major theme of *The Grapes of Wrath.* Throughout the novel, Steinbeck pays close attention to the fact that, in the battle between the haves and the have-nots, the poor usually find themselves pitted against one another rather than against the rich.

The theme of riding expands in the chapters that follow the introduction of Tom Joad. The idea of the hitchhiker on a company truck presents the difficulty of getting a free ride in a capitalist system built upon the exploitation of labor. *Chapter Three* connects this symbolism to the naturalist struggle for survival as it follows a slow-moving turtle's ill-fated attempt to cross a highway. One car swerves to avoid the turtle, but the driver of another truck aims to crush the animal upon the road. The turtle itself becomes a symbol for the poor Okies who, once forced off their land, pack everything they own onto a single truck and crawl toward California.

Chapters Four through Six present the plight of the tenant farmer in Oklahoma during the Great Depression. Tom finds that his family has deserted its farm and moved in with a nearby relative, Uncle John. Large land companies and banks have bought up the land and have introduced tractors to the area. The tractor can outplow a single farmer tenfold. Pushed off their property, the farmers seek someone upon whom to vent their anger. But the bank agents live in faraway cities and the operator of the tractor is the son of one of their neighbors who only took the job in order to keep his family from starving.

Tom meets two other wanderers as he searches around the countryside for his parents: Jim Casy, a lapsed preacher, and Muley Graves, a man who refuses to leave the land into which he poured his soul. The three of them together remember the hard times that had been the daily tenor of their lives before the advent of the tractor. They recall an almost barren world, without luxury, where farmers forged a social solidarity out of the competition for scarce resources. Time was, if a man left his house for a week, the neighbors would scavenge and dismantle it entirely. They feel that the now-deserted land still rightly belongs to them. The exchange of title deeds in some city bank is immaterial compared to the blood and sweat that the tenant farmers poured into the land. Ownership, they argue in Marxist tones, comes from working one's own hands in the dirt. Muley's stubborn vigil over a dying way of life has turned him half-crazy, and he haunts the empty shacks and dusty fields like a lonely ghost. He tells Tom and Casy that the Joad family is packing up its belongings in order to move to California, but he has refused to leave. He believes that he must stay and pester the men who have alienated him from his land.

In **Chapters Seven through Eleven** Tom is reunited with his family and helps it prepare for its trek across the country. Tom is surprised to see that his younger brother Al and his younger sister Rose of Sharon have grown into adults. Rose of Sharon has married a neighbor, Connie Rivers, and is already pregnant. The two youngest children, Ruthie and Winfield, were only babies when Tom last saw them. And the oldest son in the family, Noah, remains as strange as ever.

The Joads have sold off everything they own in order to buy a used truck and to stockpile cash for expenses on the journey. They have heard rumors that California is a land of plenty, where cotton fields and trees laden with all kinds of fruit beckon for workers' hands. Ma Joad does not quite believe that such a utopia exists, but dire situation calls for some sort of action. Worried that things may not be better there and yet unwilling to upset Pa and the children, she faces the prospect of an uncertain future with a calm but firm demeanor. Tom identifies in his mother's eyes an expression that is close to what he wore in prison.

The stoicism of Tom and Ma coheres with Reverend Casy's loss of faith. In **Chapter Eight** Granma Joad asks Casy to say grace over the family's first breakfast together, but he says that he has lost the ability to preach. Granma insists and so Casy tries to work up a short, fiery sermon about how he went into the wilderness like Jesus to try to understand the hardships of the tenant farmers. But the sermon falls flat. He says he has resigned himself to a love of humanity and the simple things in life rather than worrying about what is meant by the word "holy." The dignity of the basic necessities in life—food, water, and shelter—as opposed to high-minded ideals take on ever greater importance as the novel progresses.

Profiteers arrive to buy up the Okies' possessions at cheap prices. The Okies cannot haggle because they are desperate and in a hurry. Often a farmer trades in his team of mules and all his farm implements for a worn-out jalopy that will barely make it across the county line before breaking down. Al Joad, who worked in a garage, manages to purchase a truck in relatively good condition. Al very much wants to meet the approval of his family and particularly of Tom, who learned all about truck repair while in prison.

The Joads hold a family meeting to discuss the trip and whether Casy should be allowed to join them. Steinbeck makes much of the masculine hierarchy in the family, but it is on Ma's insistence that a person has to help a fellow man that they decide to include Casy. The Joads rush through the rest of the preparations for the trip. They load the truck with mattresses and kitchen supplies and buy enough oil to keep the motor running. The men slaughter the pigs and the women salt the meat and place it in barrels. But when they are about to set off for California, Grampa, who has always been cantankerous, refuses to go. The rough and ragged life of the tenant farmer is the only one he knows. Tom and Ma drug him to sleep and they load him atop the truck. Tom decides to go even though it means breaking the terms of his parole. The Joads set out for Route 66, the grand highway to the West Coast.

Chapters Twelve through Seventeen record their migration across the United States. In maplike detail, the Joads make their way from rest stop to gas station to campsite. They pass other Okies whose trucks have broken down, and they hear from one gas station attendant about families trading children's dolls for a gallon of gas. Casy explains to the attendant that these people are "movin' 'cause they got to. That's why folks always move. Movin' 'cause they want somepin better'n what they got." The Joads are proud of the fact that they can pay their way to California.

One evening on the road they pull over next to a couple, Ivy and Sairy Wilson, whose truck has broken down. Ivy does not know how to fix the engine, so, low on money, they are stuck where they are. After the Joads clamber down to make camp for the evening Grampa has a stroke. The Wilsons immediately offer their tent for him to lie in, and he soon dies in their bed. A bond forms between the two families as they bury Grampa and eat a funeral feast of salt pork and potatoes. Worried that someone might find Grampa's body and think he had been murdered, Tom writes a short obituary and appends an epitaph from the Psalms, "Blessed is he whose transgression is forgiven, whose sin is covered." Rose of Sharon worries that the stress of travel and the sight of death may affect the health of her unborn baby; but only Connie listens to her troubles. In order to thank the Wilsons for their help but also to spare the strain on their overloaded truck, the Joads offer to repair the Wilsons' truck. Tom and Al run back into the nearest town to buy some spare parts so that they can fix the engine. At the junkyard they meet a one-eyed man who is rotten with alcohol and self-pity. Tom sternly tells him to quit his complaining and comport himself with more dignity. They pay for the parts and return to repair the truck. The next day both families set out on their exodus west in a two-vehicle caravan.

The Joads and the Wilsons travel along with thousands of other families who are heading to California in a modern-day wagon train. In scenes that mix a lyric list of midcentury Americana with a muscular sentimentalism, Okies beg for food and water at roadside restaurants and build tent cities. Route 66 is a place where professional truck drivers are the gallant knights of the road, where chocolate cream and pineapple cream pies are staples, and where people play nickel slot machines in hopes of a quick payoff. In a particularly pathetic scene in **Chapter Fifteen,** a migrating farmer tries to buy a loaf of bread for 10 cents. When he learns that the loaf costs 15 cents he asks the waitress to cut 10-cents worth off for him. She refuses until a regular customer, a truck driver, chastises her for being hard-hearted. To make amends she turns to the farmer's kids, who stare up at her with large, puppy dog eyes, and sells them expensive candy as if it only cost a penny. When the truck driver follows the Okies out of the restaurant he leaves a tip large enough to cover the cost of the candy and then some.

As the Joads near California they begin to hear stories that differ from their belief that it is the promised land. At one campsite in **Chapter Sixteen** a ragged man tells them of the fierce competition for jobs and the miserable living conditions there. He lived there for a year before deciding to head back east. He prophesies that it will be the same for people like the Joads, that they will not find much work and that they will get hungrier and hungrier until "they'll work for nothin' but biscuits." Chagrined but not dissuaded, the Joads and the Wilsons press on to the edge of the desert.

They reach Needles, California, in **Chapter Eighteen.** With only the desert between them and the lush green valleys around Bakersfield, they stop to gather strength before a final push to their destination. The men find momentary bliss when they bathe the dust of the road off them in a nearby river. But they meet another man on his way back to the east. He tells them about the hordes of migrant workers whom the large landowners exploit, and how millions of acres lie fallow because the owners will not allow people to work them. Noah Joad decides he would rather stay by this river and live off its fish than risk the disappointments that might lie ahead. He wanders off and leaves the family at its camp. Sairy Wilson falls ill and Ivy tells the Joads to go on without them.

They cross the desert at night and meet guards outside of Bakersfield. The guards want to inspect the truck for fruit and vegetables that might contain insects, but Ma refuses to let them climb up on top. She tells them that Granma is sick and holds her head up to show her grimaced face. The guards relent and tell Tom where the nearest doctor is. When they pass on the family marvels at the beauty of the landscape. Fruit trees, green fields, and crystal-clear air abound. But Ma looks completely worn out; this worries Tom until she confesses that Granma is already dead. Ma kept the guards off the truck because she thought they might not let them in if they knew Granma was dead. Casy marvels at Ma's strength to lie next to a dead woman, and Rose of Sharon worries yet again that the closeness of death may affect her fetus.

The Joads settle briefly in Hooverville, a semipermanent campsite for migrant workers. Floyd Knowles, who had been in California for a while, informs them of the basic way of life in the area. He tells them about the trap of poverty, where the hunger of your children and your own sense of survival will force you to swallow your pride and work for almost nothing. Some folk, he says, get "bull-simple" from getting pushed around by the police too much, and outspoken workers who demand fair treatment will find themselves blacklisted. Tom at first does not trust Floyd's advice, but when a contractor comes from Tulare County to offer work, Tom sees how shifty the owners can be. Floyd asks for a written contract, but the man refuses to provide one and then has the police arrest Floyd as a suspected communist. Floyd hits the deputy and runs away. The deputy tries to shoot him but hits a woman in the hand by mistake. Casy and Tom strike down the deputy, and then Casy tells Tom to hide so his family will not get into trouble. When more police arrive Casy takes the rap and is hauled away.

This scene represents the turning point of two major themes of the novel. The Joad men appear broken by the bitter reality of life in California. Their blank-faced, stubborn stoicism in the face of predictable failure appears outdated here. Uncle John's reaction to the disappointment is to go on a drinking binge because "a fella got to do what he got to. Nobody don' know enough to tell 'im." Ma responds to this remnant of rugged individualism with disgust and anger. Rallying her strength to a renewed feistiness, she tells the men to pull together as a family. A feminine interest in the survival of the community overwhelms the self-interest of the men. Tom, for his part, responds to his mother's wishes by tracking down his inebriated uncle and knocking him unconscious to bring him back to the truck. But Rose of Sharon's husband, Connie, strikes out on his own. He abandons the Joads' stubborn pursuit of farmwork in favor of the opportunities in the city.

The entire California section of the novel represents a study in different forms of community. From Hooverville the Joads head south to a government camp in Weedpatch. Unlike the improvised community at Hooverville, which is always subject to owner-led raids, the camp in Weedpatch maintains its own order. The Joads live there from **Chapters Twenty-two through Twenty-five.** The government camp presents a respite from the harsh conditions forced upon migrant workers. The camp manager, Jim Rawley, takes a special interest in their comfort, and the Joads take pleasure in the luxury of indoor plumbing and hot showers. Founded upon socialist principles, the camp is run by committees. Direct charity from one family to another is forbidden, but those who have extra food and clothes may contribute to the camp councils, which then dispense the goods to the needier members of the community. A Ladies

Committee tells Ma Joad about the various chores required of a family if it wishes to join the camp. This scene argues for the priority of the group over the will of the individual, with a particular emphasis upon the belief that traditional domesticity should serve as the model for social coalitions.

Each of the chapters in this section of the novel rehearses the idea that cooperation is better than competition. Two other members of the camp, Timothy and Wilkie Wallace, help Tom Joad get a job even though it takes work out of their hands. Their employer, Mr. Thomas, espouses a similar belief when he complains about the owner-led conspiracy to lower the wage price. Even one of the Joad children, Ruthie, learns the hard way about the vices of individualism. A member of the Ladies Committee scolds her when she tries to break into a game of croquet before her turn.

The ultimate example of cooperative spirit occurs in **Chapter Twenty-four** at the government camp dance. A regular and popular affair, it attracts workers from all over. Mr. Thomas warns the Wallaces and Tom that the local owners have paid some farmers to make trouble at the dance so that the police can raid the camp and destroy it. Careful planning and nonviolent measures, however, thwart the plan, and the dance is as successful as usual. One of the ironies of this scene is that the troublemakers are out-of-work farmers, just like many members of the camp; another is that the insistence upon a nonviolent response to violence proves to be, later in the novel, a hard lesson for Tom to learn.

Chapter Twenty-five is the thematic abstract of the novel. There Steinbeck provides a summary of the exploitations of the working class. He denigrates the hoarding of property and laments the fact that land lies wastefully fallow. The profligate waste by the owners robs the masses of their sustenance. Out of this comes a powerful image of ripening anger, of the grapes of wrath that are growing on the vine. The chapter suggests that the workers are on the verge of a revolution.

Despite the amenities of the government camp, the Joads finally leave because they cannot find work in the area. Near starvation, they head north, in **Chapter Twenty-six,** to pick peaches at the Hooper ranch. When they approach the ranch they are stopped by police who tell them to wait for an escort. The police guide them past picketers who line the road outside of the ranch. Tom wonders what they are protesting but decides to wait until later to find out. A foreman points the Joads toward a filthy ramshackle house and then tells them to get to work. Ma and Rose of Sharon try to clean up the house while the men and children pick peaches. Ma then goes to the company store to buy food for dinner and learns that it charges higher than normal prices and that the clerk refuses to extend credit. Tom works as fast as possible to earn money but is told that his first bushel is worthless because he bruised the peaches. After a long, hard day the Joads garner just enough money to pay for a single night's food. Ma buys a can of milk for Winfield, who has collapsed because of starvation. Rose of Sharon complains that she needs milk for her coming baby. Ma agrees but tells her that she has to take care of the nearly dying first. When Winfield recovers, Ma offers the rest of the milk to her daughter.

After dinner Tom decides to sneak past the fence to ask the picketers about their grievance. He asks Al and Pa to go, but Pa is dead tired and Al wants to chase after women. Tom manages to avoid gun-toting guards at the ranch's outer fence and finds the picketers camping in a nearby culvert. To his surprise, their leader is Jim Casy. Casy tells Tom how he has realized that his mission is to organize the workers against the wage gouging of the owners. If the laborers unite they will seize power away from the owners and be able to demand fair wages. He predicts that the price per bushel will decline tomorrow now that Hooper has smuggled in new workers. Then, just as Tom begins to mull over his options, a band of hired thugs descends upon them and clubs Casy to death. Half in revenge and half in self-protection, Tom wrestles a club away from a thug and crushes his skull. Beaten but alive, Tom sneaks back inside the ranch, where he hides in the Joads' house.

The next day Casy's prediction proves true; Hooper lowers the wage per bushel from 5 cents to 2 cents. The Joads decide to leave and smuggle Tom out under some mattresses in the back of the truck. Short on food and at the end of their strength, they happen across a farm in need of cotton pickers. As one of the earliest arrivals they have the privilege of living in a clean, dry boxcar. Pa becomes more optimistic, since he grew up picking cotton in Oklahoma. The scenes in **Chapter Twenty-eight** reprise life back East before the dust bowl in that the Joads can earn enough money to live with dignity. They buy new clothes and can afford to eat meat every night of the week. Al, Pa, and Uncle John work while Tom hides out in the bushes down the river from the camp.

The Joads share their boxcar with the Wainwright family. Al and the Wainwrights' daughter Aggie fall in love and disappear every evening to make love. Mrs. Wainwright approaches Ma about her son's intentions, but Al prevents a scandal by announcing that he and Aggie are engaged. The two families unite in their joy and celebrate with a meal of sweetened pancakes. Al then informs the families that he and Aggie intend to strike out for the city, where he hopes to get a job as a mechanic. Aggie's last name (which literally means a fixer of wagons) suggests that this is an appropriate destiny. But Ma forestalls the move by insisting that Al stay with the family until the cotton-picking season is over.

The lives of the children, Ruthie and Winfield, represent a microcosm of the social conditions in each of these communities. Whereas in Weedpatch they played games under the supervision of a member of the Ladies Committee, they must pick peaches at the Hooper ranch and pick cotton at this latest spot. The spirit of cooperation also disappears once they move away from the government camp. With some of the extra money the Joads have earned in the cotton fields, Ma buys Cracker Jacks for Ruthie and Winfield. But when Ruthie refuses to share hers with the other children a larger girl steals them from her. Overwrought at the loss of her treat, Ruthie yells at the larger girl that her brother is a murderer and he will kill the girl. Winfield runs to tell Ma that Ruthie has revealed Tom's presence.

Ma realizes that the family cannot help Tom any longer and that he will have to take care of himself from now on. Throughout the novel Ma struggles to keep the family together, but the grinding forces of exploitation and poverty continue to rip it asunder. From the loss of the grandparents to Noah's and Connie's disappearances to Al's marriage, *The Grapes of Wrath* is a story of the disintegration of the Joad family. Resigned to the loss of Tom, she slips down the river toward Tom's hideout. She tells Tom that he has to leave or else risk discovery. He understands. The death of Casy and his own time alone in the wilderness have sobered him. He tells Ma that he will spend his life trying to improve the plight of the working class. He plans to take up Casy's vocation to organize the people against the owners.

The cotton season comes to an end. **Chapters Twenty-nine and Thirty,** the last two of the novel, record the onset of a rainy winter. The river begins to rise over its banks just as Rose of Sharon goes into labor. Pa Joad organizes the other men to build a levee to protect the camp from flooding. For a short while they succeed, but their efforts eventually prove futile as the river inundates the area around the boxcars. The water swamps the Joads' truck and they are forced to live atop a wooden platform in the boxcar in order to stay above the waterline. The desolation outside mirrors the bleakness inside as Rose of Sharon's baby is stillborn.

Once more Ma makes the best she can out of a desperate situation. She decides to head for higher, drier ground where Rose of Sharon can recover her strength. She leaves Al behind with Aggie and the Joads' possessions and sets out with Pa, Uncle John, Ruthie, Winfield, and Rose of Sharon. Here in the last few pages of the novel Steinbeck conveys their plight through the heavy symbolism of Ruthie's and Rose of Sharon's different reactions to the needs of the group.

As they walk across the land, Ruthie picks a "scraggly geranium gone wild" and places a rain-soaked petal upon her nose. Winfield begs her for a petal to place on his nose, but she refuses. A fight ensues. Ma intervenes and demands that Ruthie give Winfield a petal. She complies by jabbing one onto Winfield's nose and then cursing him. With the joy of singular possession of the flower now removed, she resignedly hands it entirely over to her brother. Ruthie has yet to learn the value of community.

The rain picks up again and the Joads run into an old barn. Here they find a young boy and an old man who is on the verge of death from starvation. The boy provides a dry blanket for Rose of Sharon, who is still weak from her labor, and he then tells Ma that the old man is too weak even to eat. The old man's lips move and Ma bends down to put her ear to his mouth to hear his words. She tells him she will take care of him as soon as she gets her daughter into the dry blanket. The boy cries out again that the old man is dying, that he is starving to death. Ma quiets him and looks around the barn at her tired family. Pa and Uncle John look blankly at the old man. But Rose of Sharon's eyes meet Ma's. Rose of Sharon looks at her mother for a moment, and then she says, "Yes." Ma smiles and says to her daughter, "I knowed you would." They understand one another as mothers for the first time. As if they have formed their own Ladies Committee, they will do whatever they can to help the group survive. Ma tells the boy and the rest of her family to go into the toolshed and leave her daughter alone with the old man. After they leave, Rose of Sharon gathers her strength and then approaches the old man. She bares her milk-laden breast to him and tells him he has got to eat. She squirms closer and pulls his head to her breast and he begins to nurse. She holds him there, stroking his hair, and looks across the barn with a mysterious smile upon her face. ❖

—*Jonathan Fortescue*
Harvard University

List of Characters

Tom Joad, although he killed a man with a shovel during a drunken fight, remains the apple of his family's eye. His large, muscular hands and his tight-lipped expression suggest the willfulness and the squelched anger that make him the main source of strength in the family as they head West. His skill at engine repair, which he learned in prison, makes him indispensable to their pilgrimage. But Tom's instinct for laconic self-preservation makes him somewhat slow to see the larger interests of the Okies. Doomed to murder again, he is forced into an exile from his own family.

Ma Joad, worn out from years of toil and dust, grows feistier as the novel progresses. Able to adapt more quickly to the loss of their land, she concentrates on keeping her family whole. A stalwart homemaker, she makes do with the barest essentials and reminds the men of their duty to provide for the family.

Pa Joad (Tom Joad, Sr.) is strong, stubborn, and illiterate, and knows only how to shoulder his plight rather than how to change it. His sense of self-worth gradually erodes as he becomes a pawn of large landowners in California.

Al Joad shares many qualities of his older brother Tom. Deeply admiring Tom's reputation as a killer, he copies many of his mannerisms. He intuitively grasps the archaism of tenant farming and realizes that a better life may be found as a mechanic in the city. He agrees to marry Aggie Wainwright (whose name suggests his desired occupation) near the end of the novel and leaves the Joad family.

Uncle John Joad, obsessed with his own sinfulness, represses his desires for liquor, women, and food until he bursts into a spasmodic pursuit of each. He goes out of his way to be kind to children in order to atone for the death of his wife, who died of an ectopic pregnancy. Much like Pa Joad, he is too old to change his ways in the new world of tractor farming.

Rose of Sharon Joad, the younger sister of Tom, is married to Connie Rivers. The course of her pregnancy throughout the novel traces the symbolic decline of the Joad family. Her whining and fretting give way to a womanly resolve, particularly after her husband abandons her. She gives birth during season-al flooding to a stillborn and then nurses a starving elderly man with her milk.

Ruthie and *Winfield Joad* are the younger Joad children. They depend on the adults in the family to see them through each crisis. They fear the indoor plumbing of the government camp. Winfield almost starves to death, and Ruthie accidentally reveals that Tom is wanted for murder.

Granma and Grampa Joad are relics from the past of long-term tenant farming. Grampa fought Indians. Both die on the way to California.

Jim Casy ia a preacher who has lost his faith. Once capable of fire and brimstone sermons, he retreated into the wilderness to wrestle with his beliefs. Upon his return he espouses a love for humanity rather than a spiritual longing for God. He hitches a ride with the Joads to California and sacrifices himself to save the family from the police. Later Tom Joad finds Casy leading the drive to organize a union. Hired thugs kill Casy and Tom avenges his death.

Connie Rivers moves with the Joads to California but soon abandons their stubborn attempt to make it as farmers on the West Coast. He speaks of working in the city and living like a dandy before leaving his pregnant wife, Rose of Sharon, with her family.

Muley Graves's name suggests his character. A symbol for the dying age of animal-powered agriculture, he haunts the vacant shacks of the dispossessed tenant farmers in Oklahoma. He bids the Joads farewell and stays behind in Oklahoma to grow steadily crazier in his vengeful isolation.

Ivy and Sairy Wilson, fellow travelers on the road to California, help the Joads bury Grampa. Tom fixes their truck and the two families journey along Route 66 together. Sairy's strength gives out before they cross the desert and Wilson insists the Joads leave them behind.

Floyd Knowles speaks out against the hiring tactics of the farm owners when a contractor comes to Hooverville. The police and the contractor accuse him of being a communist, and he is forced to flee.

Jim Rawley is manager of the Weedpatch Government Camp, a self-regulating campground for migrant workers. His supervision of the camp comes closest to a socialist ideal of personal dignity with community commonwealth. He avoids violence and confrontation.

Mr. Thomas is a sympathetic landowner who labors beside his hired hands. He explains to Tom how larger corporate interests control the wage rate. He also warns the government camp of an impending raid. ✤

Critical Views

CHRISTOPHER ISHERWOOD ON *THE GRAPES OF WRATH* AS PROPAGANDA

[Christopher Isherwood (1904–1986) was a celebrated British novelist and playwright; among his works are *Goodbye to Berlin* (1939) and *A Meeting by the River* (1967). In this review of *The Grapes of Wrath,* Isherwood voices a complaint that many have made about the novel and about Steinbeck's work generally: that it is too propagandistic and too obvious in its social criticism.]

Readers of the earlier novels and stories do not need to be reminded that Mr. Steinbeck is a master of realistic writing—a master among masters, for America is extraordinarily rich in his peculiar kind of talent. In the presence of such powers, such observation, such compassion, such humor, it seems almost ungrateful to make reservations—to ask that what is so good should be even better. But a writer of Mr. Steinbeck's caliber can only be insulted by mere praise; for his defects are as interesting as his merits. What are these defects? Why isn't *The Grapes of Wrath* entirely satisfying as a work of art?

It is a mark of the greatest poets, novelists and dramatists that they all demand a high degree of cooperation from their audience. The form may be simple, and the language plain as daylight, but the inner meaning, the latent content of a masterpiece will not be perceived without a certain imaginative and emotional effort. In this sense, the great artist makes every one of his readers into a philosopher and poet, to a greater or lesser degree, according to that reader's powers. The novelist of genius, by presenting the particular instance, indicates the general truth. He indicates, but he does not attempt to state it—for to state the general truth is to circumscribe it, to make it somewhat less than itself. The final verdict, the ultimate synthesis, must be left to the reader; and each reader will modify it in accordance with his needs. The aggregate of all these individual syntheses is the measure of the impact of a work of art upon the world. It is, in fact, a part of that work. In this way, masterpieces, throughout the ages, actually undergo a sort of organic growth.

At this point arises the problem of the so-called propaganda-novel, and the often-repeated question: "Can propaganda produce good art?" "All art is propaganda," the propagandists retort—and, of course, in a sense, they are right. Novels inevitably reflect contemporary conditions. But here the distinction appears. In a successful work of art, the "propaganda" (which means, ultimately, the appeal to the tribunal of humanity) has been completely digested, it forms part of the latent content; its conclusions are left to the conscience and judgment of the reader himself. In an imperfect work of art, however, the "propaganda" is overt. It is stated, and therefore limited. The novelist becomes a schoolmaster.

Mr. Steinbeck, in his eagerness for the cause of the share-croppers and his indignation against the wrongs they suffer, has been guilty, throughout this book, of such personal, school-masterish intrusions upon the reader. Too often, we feel him at our elbow, explaining, interpreting, interfering with our own independent impressions. And there are moments at which Ma Joad and Casy—otherwise such substantial figures—seem to fade into mere mouthpieces, as the author's voice comes through, like another station on the radio. All this is a pity. It seriously impairs the total effect of the novel, brilliant, vivid, and deeply moving as it is. The reader has not been allowed to cooperate, and he comes away vaguely frustrated.

Overt political propaganda, however just in its conclusions, must always defeat its own artistic ends, for this very reason: the politicosociological case is general, the artistic instance is particular. If you claim that your characters' misfortunes are due to the existing System, the reader may retort that they are actually brought about by the author himself. Legally speaking, it was Mr. Steinbeck who murdered Casy and killed Grampa and Granma Joad. In other words, fiction is fiction. Its truths are parallel to, but not identical with the truths of the real world.

Mr. Steinbeck still owes us a great novel. He has everything which could produce it—the technical ability, the fundamental seriousness, the sympathy, the vision. There are passages in this book which achieve greatness. The total artistic effect falls short of its exciting promise. *The Grapes of Wrath* is a milestone in American fiction, but I do not believe that it represents the height of its author's powers.

—Christopher Isherwood, "The Tragedy of Eldorado," *Kenyon Review* 1, No. 4 (Autumn, 1939): 452–53

HARRY THORNTON MOORE ON STEINBECK'S DIALOGUE

[Harry Thornton Moore (1908–1981) was a leading scholar on D. H. Lawrence; he edited many of Lawrence's works and wrote an important biography, *The Priest of Love* (1974). He taught for many years at Southern Illinois University. In this extract, from an early monograph on Steinbeck, Moore studies the dialogue in *The Grapes of Wrath,* finding it artificial precisely because of its naturalism.]

Things people say in *The Grapes of Wrath* sometimes have a flavor of staginess because Steinbeck was trying to reproduce speech exactly. This presents a problem: complete literalness in such matters doesn't necessarily simulate life in literature. American speech has been successfully fused into creative prose by perhaps only one writer, Ernest Hemingway. Hemingway doesn't attempt literalness, but adapts the rudiments of American speech-rhythm to his personal sense of cadence. He is monotonous and repetitious, but deliberately so, and with telling effect. Although the speeches of his people have sufficient relation to their source so they could be fitted to American lips, they are nevertheless not automatic reproduction—they have their own identity. These speeches are Hemingway's own distinctive instrument and at the same time a living suggestion of American utterance. The most successful speech-reproductions in *The Grapes of Wrath* are when Steinbeck approximates this condition in the chapters where he is trying to convey a general effect rather than literal individual conversations. These chapters occur at frequent intervals throughout the book; they are devoted to generalized accounts of the moving body of people, of the factors that drove them forth, of the topography of their journey, of what they will find at the end of it. These sections are in some respects the best in the book; they never quite function so efficiently as they should because the contrapuntal chapters about the Joad family don't always have the continuous strength to carry them. If the central narrative were more forcefully concentrated, these choral chapters would be set off magnificently, given more meaning and volume. But although they don't realize their full accessory value, still they have a power in the way they catch the essential spirit of that sprawling westering movement. And they pick out its vocal overtones; there is at times a resemblance to Carl Sandburg's *The People, Yes*. American names are named, places are mentioned, automobiles and native foods are identified. And all this is not literal speech reproduction, but a swelling musical suggestion of it that gives a far greater sense of "reality" than literal reporting. These chapters have an American resonance.

—Harry Thornton Moore, *The Novels of John Steinbeck: A First Critical Study* (Chicago: Normandie House, 1939), pp. 59–60

FREDERIC I. CARPENTER ON JIM CASY AS PHILOSOPHER

[Frederic I. Carpenter (1903–1991) was a prolific literary critic, having written monographs on Robinson Jeffers (1962), Laurens Van der Post (1969), and Eugene O'Neill (1979). He taught at the University of Chicago, Harvard, and the University of California at Berkeley. In this extract from an important early article on *The Grapes of Wrath,* Carpenter studies the novel from a philosophical perspective, finding in Jim Casy's attitude to nature a religious transcendentalism reminiscent of Ralph Waldo Emerson.]

"Ever know a guy that said big words like that?" asks the truck driver in the first narrative chapter of *The Grapes of Wrath.* "Preacher," replies Tom Joad. "Well, it makes you mad to hear a guy use big words. Course with a preacher it's all right because nobody would fool around with a preacher anyway." But soon afterward Tom meets Jim Casy and finds him changed. "I was a preacher," said the man seriously, "but not no more." Because Casy has ceased to be an orthodox minister and no longer uses big words, Tom Joad plays around with him. And the story results.

But although he is no longer a minister, Jim Casy continues to preach. His words have become simple and his ideas unorthodox. "Just Jim Casy now. Ain't got the call no more. Got a lot of sinful idears—but they seem kinda sensible." A century before, this same experience and essentially these same ideas had occurred to another preacher: Ralph Waldo Emerson had given up the ministry because of his unorthodoxy. But Emerson had kept on using big words. Now Casy translates them: "Why do we got to hang it on God or Jesus? Maybe it's all men an' all women we love; maybe that's the Holy Sperit—the human sperit—the whole shebang. Maybe all men got one big soul ever'body's a part of." And so the Emersonian oversoul comes to earth in Oklahoma.

Unorthodox Jim Casy went into the Oklahoma wilderness to save his soul. And in the wilderness he experienced the religious feeling of identity with nature which has always been the heart of transcendental mysticism: "There was the hills, an' there was me, an' we wasn't separate no more. We was one thing. An' that one thing was holy." Like Emerson, Casy came to the conviction that holiness, or goodness, results from this feeling of unity: "I got to thinkin' how we was holy when we was one thing, an' mankin' was holy when it was one thing."

Thus far Jim Casy's transcendentalism has remained vague and apparently insignificant. But the corollary of this mystical philosophy is that any man's self-seeking destroys the unity or "holiness" of nature: "An' it [this one thing] on'y got unholy when one mis'able little fella got the bit in his teeth, an' run off his own way. . . . Fella like that bust the holiness." Or, as Emerson phrased it, while discussing Nature: "The world lacks unity because man is disunited with himself. . . . Love is its demand." So Jim Casy preaches the religion of love.

He finds that this transcendental religion alters the old standards: "Here's me that used to give all my fight against the devil 'cause I figured the devil was the enemy. But they's somepin worse'n the devil got hold a the country." Now, like Emerson, he almost welcomes "the dear old devil." Now he fears not the lusts of the flesh but rather the lusts of the spirit. For the abstract lust of possession isolates a man from his fellows and destroys the unity of nature and the love of man. As Steinbeck writes: "The quality of owning freezes you forever into 'I,' and cuts you off forever from the 'we.'" Or, as the Concord farmers in Emerson's poem "Hamatreya" had exclaimed: "'Tis mine, my children's and my name's," only to have "their avarice cooled like lust in the chill of the grave." To a preacher of the oversoul, possessive egotism may become the unpardonable sin.

If a society has adopted "the quality of owning" (as typified by absentee ownership) as its social norm, then Protestant nonconformity may become the highest virtue, and even resistance to authority may become justified. At the beginning of his novel Steinbeck had suggested this, describing how "the faces of the watching men lost their bemused perplexity and became hard and angry and resistant. Then the women knew that they were safe . . . their men were whole." For this is the paradox of Protestantism: when men resist unjust and selfish authority, they themselves become "whole" in spirit.

But this American ideal of nonconformity seems negative: how can men be sure that their Protestant rebellion does not come from the devil? To this there has always been but one answer—faith: faith in the instincts of the common man, faith in ultimate social progress, and faith in the direction in which democracy is moving. So Ma Joad counsels the discouraged Tom: "Why, Tom, we're the people that live. They ain't gonna wipe us out. Why, we're the people—we go on." And so Steinbeck himself affirms a final faith in progress: "When theories change and crash, when schools, philosophies . . . grow and disintegrate, man reaches, stumbles forward. . . . Having stepped forward, he may slip back, but only half a step, never the full step back." Whether this be democratic faith, or mere transcendental optimism, it has always been the motive force of our American life and finds reaffirmation in this novel.

—Frederic I. Carpenter, "The Philosophical Joads," *College English* 2, No. 4 (January, 1941): 316–18

Maxwell Geismar on Steinbeck's Sentimentality

[Maxwell Geismar (1909–1979) was a leading American critic and biographer. Among his books are *American Moderns, from Rebellion to Conformity* (1958), *Henry James and the Jacobites* (1963), and *Mark Twain: An American Prophet* (1970). In this extract, Geismar disparages *The Grapes of Wrath* for being crippled by sentimentality.]

The inequalities of the American social system are affecting thousands of fine American families. Hence the Joads must be a fine American family. Around them Steinbeck weaves his typical fantasies, so that the Joads emerge as idealized in their own way as those smooth personages who dwell everlastingly in the pages of the *Saturday Evening Post*. Of them, of course, Ma Joad is the guiding spirit, the soul of American motherhood, her home in the kitchen but her spirit in the heavens. Like Slim and Mac she is wise, courageous, indomitable, though in tatters:

> Her hazel eyes seemed to have experienced all possible tragedy and to have mounted pain and suffering like steps into a high calm and a superhuman understanding. . . . And from her great and humble position in the family she had taken dignity and clean calm beauty. From her position as healer, her hands had grown sure and cool and quiet; from her position as arbiter she had become as remote and faultless in judgment as a goddess.

Steinbeck's sentimentality has overwhelmed him, his reliance on rhapsody rather than reflection, the violence which characterizes his temperament here turned into idyllic abstraction—

these traits which as yet prevent our considering him fully among the writers whose talent he perhaps equals. And if Ma Joad is thus portrayed, what can we say of Rose of Sharon, with her ripe voluptuousness, her drowsing aroma of universal fertility—except that this is again sentimentalized projection. Connie Rivers, in turn, reminds us of Curley's wife, and the philosophic witch of the *Cup of Gold* as a symbol of Steinbeck's sexual fascination. Noah Joad belongs to Steinbeck's hobgoblins, and Grampa is a fusion of this and the paisanos of *Tortilla Flat:*

> He fought and argued, told dirty stories. He was as lecherous as always. . . . He drank too much when he could get it, ate too much when it was there, talked too much all the time.

And with his 'little bright eyes,' his cantankerous, mischievous little old face, Grampa Joad is too much of a typical Steinbeckian whimsicality for us ever to believe, as, in short, are most of the Joads. As in *Of Mice and Men* we have in *The Grapes of Wrath* the joining of the old and the new Steinbeck, and the older themes are marked with the deterioration which comes when an author retraces without belief the patterns of his past. It is hard to believe that even Steinbeck himself accepts the Joads as people, or that he has thrown in the variety of pagan, weird, earthy, violent concepts for more than their picturesque value. *The Grapes of Wrath,* in short, often represents the dubious nuptials of *Tobacco Road* with the *Ladies' Home Journal.* But the marriage is one of convenience.

—Maxwell Geismar, "John Steinbeck: Of Wrath or Joy," *Writers in Crisis: The American Novel between Two Wars* (Boston: Houghton Mifflin, 1942), pp. 263–65

LEWIS GANNETT ON STEINBECK'S STATE OF MIND

[Lewis Gannett (1891–1966) was a journalist and critic. He wrote *Cream Hill: Discoveries of a Week-End Countryman* (1949) and translated Hjalmar Schacht's

The End of Reparations (1931). In this extract, Gannett uses Steinbeck's letters to portray the author's state of mind prior to writing *The Grapes of Wrath,* showing how his outrage at the conditions of the migrant workers' camps led directly to the commencement of the novel.]

He had written a series of articles on the migrant workers for the *San Francisco News* in October, 1936, before *Of Mice and Men* was published. He had worked on the farms of his long valley long ago in his school vacations. He knew the work; he knew the people. He knew the bitternesses. He felt them in the marrow of his bones. He also had a deep affectionate sense of identification with the fruit-pickers; and he was a Californian, and he felt a responsibility.

"I must go over into the interior valleys," he wrote Elizabeth Otis in the midst of reports on work in progress. "There are five thousand families starving to death over there, not just hungry but actually starving. The government is trying to feed them and get medical attention to them, with the Fascist group of utilities and banks and huge growers sabotaging the thing all along the line, and yelling for a balanced budget. In one tent there are twenty people quarantined for small pox and two of the women are to have babies in that tent this week. I've tied into the thing from the first and I must get down there and see it and see if I can do something to knock these murderers on the heads.

"Do you know what they're afraid of? They think that if these people are allowed to live in camps with proper sanitary facilities they will organize, and that is the bugbear of the large landowner and the corporation farmer. The states and counties will give them nothing because they are outsiders. But the crops of any part of this state could not be harvested without them. . . . Talk about Spanish children. The death of children by starvation in our valleys is simply staggering. . . . I'll do what I can. . . . Funny how mean and how little books become in the face of such tragedies."

He did what he could, and returned home to dash off a book that was announced under the title *L'Affaire Lettuceburg.* And when it was done he sat down and wrote a joint letter to his agent and his publisher, a letter beautifully and painfully illustrative of Steinbeck's attitude toward his own work: "Dear Elizabeth and Pat," he began. "This is going to be a hard letter to write. I feel badly about it. You see this book is finished and it is a bad book and I must get rid of it. It can't be printed. It is bad because it isn't honest. Oh! the incidents all happened but—I'm not telling as much of the truth about them as I know. In satire you have to restrict the picture and I just can't do satire. I've written three books now that were dishonest because they were less than the best I could do. One you never saw because I burned it the day I finished it. The second was the murder novel and this is the third. The first two were written under rather frantic financial pressure, and this last one from an obligation pressure I felt. I know, you could sell possibly 30,000 copies. I know that a great many people would think they liked this book. I, myself, have built up a hole-proof argument on how and why I liked it. I can't beat the argument, but I do not like the book. And I would be doing Pat a greater injury in letting him print it than I would be destroying it. Not once in the writing of it have I felt the curious warm pleasure that comes when work is going well. My whole work drive has been aimed at making people understand each other and then I deliberately write this book, the aim of which is to cause hatred through partial understanding. My father would have called it a smart-alec book. It was full of tricks to make people ridiculous. If I can't do better I have slipped badly. And that I won't admit—yet. . . ."

So he went back to the grind, plodding his way through *The Grapes of Wrath*. For a long time the book had no title. In September, 1938, the title went to New York on a postcard, followed by a letter saying that Steinbeck liked the title "because it is a march, because it is in our own revolutionary tradition and because in reference to this book it has a large meaning. And I like it because people know the Battle Hymn who don't know the Stars and Stripes."

That autumn he was on the home stretch. "I am desperately tired," he wrote, "but I want to finish. And mean. I feel as though shrapnel were bursting about my head. I only hope the book is some good. Can't tell yet at all. And I can't tell whether it is balanced. It is a slow plodding book but I don't think that it is dull." He also didn't think it would be a popular book.

—Lewis Gannett, "John Steinbeck: Novelist at Work" (1945), *Conversations with John Steinbeck,* ed. Thomas Fensch (Jackson: University Press of Mississippi, 1988), pp. 37–39

F. W. WATT ON SUFFERING AND TRIUMPH IN *THE GRAPES OF WRATH*

[F. W. Watt (b. 1927) is a British literary critic who has coedited *Essays in English Literature from the Renaissance to the Victorian Age* (1964) and written a study of Steinbeck, from which this extract is taken. Here, Watt believes the central focus of *The Grapes of Wrath* to be its delineation of suffering and triumph over adversity.]

The primary impact of *The Grapes of Wrath* as we have it, whatever may have been true of the earlier version Steinbeck rejected, is not to make us act, but to make us understand and share a human experience of suffering and resistance.

The understanding is at several levels. At the level of characters or persons, we are invited to see the impact the experience of westering has on Tom Joad, on his mother, his sister Rose of Sharon, and on the renegade preacher Jim Casy, who goes with them to California. Casy is made to bear most explicitly the conceptual values of the novel. About these there is little mystery, for Steinbeck's method is to keep to the level of discourse of his simplest folk. When we first see Casy he is explaining to Tom Joad how he left preaching, not merely because of the lusts that plagued him, but because religious faith as he knew it seemed to set up codes of behaviour which denied human nature its proper and full expression. At first it seems his alternative is mere amorality: "There ain't no sin and there ain't no virtue. There's just stuff people do." But it becomes apparent that behind this generosity or laxity there is a different kind of ethical and religious intensity. Casy has given up the negative or legalistic aspects of Christianity to endorse its spirit; the metaphysics of Christianity he exchanges for those of Emersonian transcendentalism: "What's this call, this sperit?. . . It's love. I love people so much I'm fit to bust, sometimes." And later, "maybe it's all men and all women we love; maybe that's the Holy Sperit—the human sperit—the whole shebang. Maybe all men got one big soul ever'body's a part of." In his turn Tom Joad hears this "call" too. His return home from prison opens the novel. He has served time for a murder committed in drunken self-defence, but as the Joad family's troubles increase his patience and temper which failed him so badly once are shown to be strengthened and con-trolled as never before. After Casy has been killed and he him-self outlawed in battles with the strike-breakers, Tom moves beyond the ways of blind, personal anger and revenge to become a kind of disciple of Jim Casy (whose initials are no doubt intentionally those of Jesus Christ), setting out in a spirit of love to spread the gospel of social justice. His famous farewell to Ma Joad makes it clear that he represents not just the determination of the proletariat to organise and rebel against injustice, but a more universal and lasting humanitarian force, an aspect of the spirit of man which—the novel sug-gests—is found especially in the very humble when they band together in sympathy and mutual protection. ⟨. . .⟩

The conclusion is consciously sensational, to the embarrass-ment of readers of delicate sensibility and a strong sense of decorum. But Steinbeck's intention is clear: he wanted to end with a powerful symbol of human life persisting despite the hostility of social forms and of nature which resulted in a destructive storm, a still-born child, destitution and starvation. In humiliation, discord and chaos, life struggles and—however gross and incongruous its means—survives and is re-born out of the tempest, through human courage, choice, and love.

For all its documentary realism, its attacks on big business and its tides of social protest and indignation, the apparent reliance on a social era rapidly fading from memory, *The Grapes of Wrath* is a work of art rather than of politics or sociology. Undoubtedly the effort to generalise and universalise has its dangers, risking sentimentality and pretentiousness, but the personal and social drama which unfolds is powerful enough to carry along these weaker moments. Despite its flaws, the novel has an imaginative power and a generosity of heart rarely equalled in American literature. With its publication in 1939 Steinbeck had set up a monument to mark the highest point of his own career, and the nadir of America's social history.

—F. W. Watt, *John Steinbeck* (New York: Grove Press, 1962), pp. 70–71, 74–75

JOSEPH FONTENROSE ON RELIGIOUS SYMBOLISM IN *THE GRAPES OF WRATH*

[Joseph Fontenrose (b. 1903), a former professor of classics at the University of California at Berkeley, has written several volumes on ancient Greek myth, including *Python: A Study of Delphic Myth and Its Origins* (1959), *The Ritual Theory of Myth* (1971), and *Orion: The Myth of the Hunter and the Huntress* (1981). In this extract from his book on Steinbeck, Fontenrose examines the varieties of religious symbolism in *The Grapes of Wrath,* finding Tom Joad to be a kind of Moses and Jim Casy a parallel to Jesus Christ.]

Tom Joad becomes the new Moses who will lead the oppressed people, succeeding Jim Casy, who had found One Big Soul in the hills, as Moses had found the Lord on Mount Horeb. As a teacher of a social gospel Casy is more like Jesus than like Moses, and nearly as many echoes of the New Testament as of the Old are heard in *The Grapes of Wrath.* Peter Lisca and Martin Shockley have listed several parallels between the Joad story and the gospel story. Jim Casy's initials are JC, and he retired to the wilderness to find spiritual truth ("I been in the hills . . . like Jesus went into the wilderness . . .") and came forth to teach a new doctrine of love and good works. One of the vigilantes who attacked him pointed him out with the words, "That's him. That shiny bastard"; and just before the mortal blow struck him Casy said, "You don' know what you're a-doin'." And Casy sacrificed himself for others when he surrendered himself as the man who had struck a deputy at Hooverville. Two Joads were named Thomas, and one became Casy's disciple, who would carry on his teaching. Tom told his mother, "I'm talkin' like Casy," after saying that he would be present everywhere, though unseen, "If Casy knowed," echoing Jesus' words, "Lo, I am with you always, . . ." Lisca and Shockley have also perceived the Eucharist in Rose of Sharon's final act, when she gave her nourishment (the body and blood) to save the life of a starving man.

The correspondences between the gospel story and Steinbeck's novel go still deeper than these critics have indicated. Thirteen persons started west, Casy and twelve Joads, who, as we have seen, also represent Judea (Judah) whom Jesus came to teach. Not only were two Joads named Thomas, but another was John; Casy's name was James, brother and disciple of Jesus. One of the twelve, Connie Rivers, was not really a Joad; he is Judas, for not only did he desert the Joads selfishly at a critical moment, but just before he did so he told his wife that he would have done better to stay home "an' study 'bout tractors. Three dollars a day they get, an' pick up extra money, too." The tractor driver of Chapter Five got three dollars a day, and the extra money was a couple of dollars for "[caving] the house in a little." Three dollars are thirty pieces of silver— remember Sinclair Lewis' Elmer Gantry, who received thirty dimes after his betrayal of the old teacher of Greek and Hebrew at the seminary. We should notice too the crowing of roosters on the night when Casy was killed—the only passage, I believe, where this is mentioned—and this at a time when the Joads had to deny Tom.

Casy taught as one with authority: "the sperit" was strong in him. His gospel coincided in certain respects with Jesus' doctrine: love for all men, sympathy for the poor and oppressed, realization of the gospel in active ministry, subordination of formal observances to men's real needs and property to humanity, and toleration of men's weaknesses and sensual desires.

When Casy said, "An' I wouldn' pray for a ol' fella that's dead. He's awright," he was saying in Okie speech, "Let the dead bury their dead" (Luke 9:60).

Casy's doctrine, however, went beyond Christ's. He had rejected the Christianity which he once preached, much as Jesus, starting out as John the Baptist's disciple, abandoned and transformed John's teachings. In *The Grapes of Wrath* John Joad, Tom's uncle, represents John the Baptist, who had practiced asceticism and emphasized remission of sins. John Joad, of course, has almost no literal resemblance to John the Baptist; but he did live a lonely, comfortless life in a spiritual desert, and he was guilt-ridden, obsessed with sin. He was a pious man, a Baptist in denomination; and we hear about his baptism "over to Polk's place. Why, he got to plungin' an' jumpin'. Jumped over a feeny bush as big as a piana. Over he'd jump, an' back he'd jump, howlin' like a dog-wolf in moon time." John, trying to atone for his "sins," was good to children, and they "thought he was Jesus Christ Awmighty." He was, however, the forerunner: for one greater than he had come. When Casy gave himself up to the officers to save Tom, then John realized how unworthy he was beside Casy: "He done her so easy. Jus' stepped up there an' says, 'I done her.' "

It is John Joad's Christianity that Casy rejected. After worrying about his sexual backslidings, Casy came to the conclusion that

> "Maybe it ain't a sin. Maybe it's just the way folks is. . . . There ain't no sin and there ain't no virtue. There's just stuff people do. It's all part of the same thing. And some of the things folks do is nice, and some ain't nice, but that's as far as any man got a right to say."

His doctrine of sin led to his positive doctrine of love: ". . . 'maybe it's all men an' all women we love; maybe that's the Holy Sperit—the human sperit—the whole shebang. Maybe all men got one big soul ever'body's a part of.' " And so he arrived at the doctrine of the Oversoul. "All that lives is holy," he said, and this meant that he should be with other men: "a wilderness ain't no good, 'cause his little piece of a soul wasn't no good 'less it was with the rest, an' was whole." In a California jail his doctrine took complete shape as a social gospel, and Casy's ministry became the organizing of farm workers into unions.

—Joseph Fontenrose, *John Steinbeck: An Introduction and Interpretation* (New York: Holt, Rinehart & Winston, 1963), pp. 78–80

HOWARD LEVANT ON ALLEGORY IN *THE GRAPES OF WRATH*

[Howard Levant (b. 1929), who has taught at Hartwick College (Oneonta, New York) and Pepperdine University (Malibu, California), has edited *The Writer and the World* (1976) and written *The Novels of John Steinbeck* (1974), from which this extract is taken. Here, Levant focuses on the turtle episode in Chapter 3 as a typical example of the use of allegory in Steinbeck's novel.]

Steinbeck is ⟨. . .⟩ scrupulous in the use of allegory as a way of universalizing an abstract particular. In his earlier work this method can produce a tangibly artificial, forced result, but allegory is a credible and functional device in *The Grapes of Wrath*. The turtle episode in Chapter III is justly famous. Objectively, we have a fully realized description of a land turtle's patient, difficult journey over dust fields, across a road and walled embankment, and on through the dust. The facts are the starting point; nature is not distorted or manipulated to yield allegorical meaning. The turtle seems awkward but it is able to survive, like the Joads, and like them it is moving southwest, out of the dry area. It can protect itself against a natural danger like the red ant it kills, as the Joads protect themselves by their unity. The turtle's eyes are "fierce, humorous," suggesting force that takes itself easily; the stronger Joads are a fierce, humorous people. When mismanaged human power attacks, as when a truck swerves to hit the turtle, luck is on the animal's side—it survives by luck. The Joads survive the mismanagement that produced the Dust Bowl and the brutalizing man-made conditions in California as much by luck as by design. The relation to the Joads of the life-bearing function of the turtle is more obscure, or perhaps overly ambitious. The factual starting point is that, unknowingly, the turtle carries an oat seed in its shell and unknowingly drops and plants the seed in the dust, where it will rest until water returns. The most obvious link in the Joad family is the pregnant Rose of Sharon, but her baby is born dead. Perhaps compassion is "born," as in Uncle John's thoughts as he floats the dead baby down the flooding river in its apple box coffin:

> Go down an' tell 'em. Go down in the street an' rot an' tell 'em that way. That's the way you can talk. . . . Maybe they'll know then.

But this appeal is strained, too greatly distanced from the factual starting point. The link works in the restricted sense that Ruthie and Winfield are "planted," and will perhaps take root, in the new environment of California. At this point the careful allegory collapses under its own weight, yet care is taken to join the device to the central narrative. In Chapter IV, Tom Joad picks up a turtle, and later Casy remarks on the tenacity of the breed:

> "Nobody can't keep a turtle though. They work at it and work at it, and at last one day they get out and away they go—off somewheres."

This recognition of the turtle's purposeful tenacity interprets and places the preceding interchapter in the central narrative. Tom calls the turtle "an old bulldozer," a figure that works in opposition to the threatening insect life the tractors suggest as self-defeating, destructive tools of "the Bank." Again, a purposeful turtle is opposed to homeless domestic animals, like the "thick-furred yellow shepherd dog" that passes Tom and Casy, to suggest precisely the ruined land and the destruction of the old ways of life on the most basic, animal level, where the wild (or free) animal survives best. These and other supporting details extend the exemplum into the narrative; they continue and deepen Steinbeck's foreshadowing, moralizing insight naturally, within the range of biological imagery. It is true, allowing for the one collapse of the allegory, that none of Steinbeck's earlier work exhibits as profound a comprehension of what can be done to "place" an allegorical narrative device.

—Howard Levant, "The Fully Matured Art: *The Grapes of Wrath*," *The Novels of John Steinbeck: A Critical Study* (Columbia: University of Missouri Press, 1974), pp. 101–3

FLOYD C. WATKINS ON STEINBECK'S IGNORANCE OF THE OKIES

[Floyd C. Watkins (b. 1920), formerly Candler Professor of American Literature at Emory University, has written *Thomas Wolfe's Characters: Portraits from Life* (1957), *The Flesh and the Word* (1971), and several books on Robert Penn Warren. In this extract, Watkins believes that Steinbeck did not sufficiently know the culture of the Okies he describes in *The Grapes of Wrath*, with the result that their humanity is destroyed.]

A character in fiction is known in part by his relationship with things; he is defined by the clutter of his world. If the things are vague or false, the character is unlikely to be genuine. In a novel with sparse details, the people usually share the vagueness of the environment. Nature may be a large part of the raw materials of fiction. When an author does not know the natural objects of the world he is writing about, then he also gets the manufactured products and the people wrong. A skyscraper or a horse trough or a churn helps to make characters what they are. A writer who does not know a world well should not write about it. But that is precisely what Californian John Steinbeck did in *The Grapes of Wrath* when he wrote about Okies, a people he did not know. ⟨. . .⟩

When *The Grapes of Wrath* violates the mores of people like the Joads, the result almost every time is a reduction of the humanity of the characters. Grampa's leaving his underwear unbuttoned and his fly open is a violation of conventions in the rural Protestant ethic, and even if he is "lecherous as always" his misbehavior would not have been tolerated by members of his family, especially the females. Pa's language before his wife and daughter seems incredibly exaggerated when he refers to his lecherous son's "nuts just a-eggin' him on." Grampa calls a brother, a daughter, and a grandson "sons-a-bitches," and that cussword is almost never taken lightly by people of his class and place. Except in foolish and drunken situations, such name-calling usually has dire consequences (as is potentially true in *Light in August* and *As I Lay Dying*). But Grampa's language provokes not even a shrug. For the sake of sensationalism, perhaps, Steinbeck momentarily forgets the abstract philosophical goodness he attributes to most of the migrants, and he does not even allow them the dignity they do possess. Granma has "survived only because she was as mean as her husband." She opposes him "with a shrill ferocious religiosity that was as lecherous and as savage as anything Grampa could offer." After she rips "one of his buttocks nearly off" with a shotgun blast, he admires her. Grampa and Granma "both sleeps in the barn." The humanity of these characters is so utterly destroyed by Steinbeck's treatment of them that no dignity can survive even when they die. They are ruined by a tone of amused tolerance of near-murder with a shotgun. And their manners at the table leave them with no measure of dignity.

> Granma said proudly, "A wicketer, cussin'er man never lived. He's goin' to hell on a poker, praise Gawd! Wants to drive the truck!" she said spitefully. "Well, he ain't goin' ta."
>
> Grampa choked, and a mouthful of paste [pork, biscuit, thick gravy] sprayed into his lap, and he coughed weakly.
>
> Granma smiled up at Tom. "Messy, ain't he?" she observed brightly.

Actually Steinbeck is demeaning his own characters whom he presumably pities and loves. He is condemning them on social grounds even though the book thematically protests economic abuse of them. At times Steinbeck's amused treatment of them is as inhumane or inhuman as the capitalists are to the migrants. Tom Joad's family are as unloving as they are illiterate when he spends four years in jail and his mother writes him only a postcard after two years and then granny sends him a Christmas card a year later. Yet the Joads should be a writing family. Witness the extensive correspondence between uneducated soldiers and their families during the Civil

War. In other incidents caricature occurs because Steinbeck, unintentionally perhaps, reveals how his poor people are unfeeling. The truck they travel in is crowded, no doubt. Yet it is implausible to take all the mattresses and barrels of pork and cooking utensils yet to be unable to find a place for the single stationery box of letters and pictures which Ma burns before she leaves. Surely she could sew the most precious into the mattresses.

—Floyd C. Watkins, "Flat Wine from *The Grapes of Wrath*," In *Time and Place: Some Origins of American Fiction* (Athens: University of Georgia Press, 1977), pp. 19, 25–26

SYLVIA JENKINS COOK ON STEINBECK'S INTEREST IN GROUP BEHAVIOR

[Sylvia Jenkins Cook (b. 1943), a professor of English at the University of Missouri at St. Louis, has written *From Tobacco Road to Route 66: The Southern Poor White in Fiction* (1976) and *Erskine Caldwell and the Fiction of Poverty* (1991). In this extract, Cook studies *In Dubious Battle* as a preface to Steinbeck's treatment of group behavior in *The Grapes of Wrath*.]

Steinbeck's interest in the phenomenon of group behavior was certainly not new to American fiction, as Mark Twain's description of the mob in *The Adventures of Huckleberry Finn* will testify: "The pitifulest thing out is a mob . . . they don't fight with courage that's born in them, but with courage that's borrowed from their mass." In the 1930s a more positive characterization of group behavior emerged in the many proletarian novels that dealt with the solidarity of the union, where workers could acquire dignity, strength, and power, all inaccessible to the exploited and impotent individual. What distinguishes Steinbeck's interest in group man from either of these examples is his reluctance to attach any moral judgment to the group phenomenon. In this original letter describing his fascination with the possible manifestations of the group, he writes that "Russia is giving us a nice example of human units who are trying with a curious nostalgia to get away from their individuality and re-establish the group unit the race remembers and wishes. I am not drawing conclusions." By the following year he had begun work on what he called "the Communist idea" which was to become *In Dubious Battle.* That Steinbeck's stated intentions for this novel are not wholly congruent with the effect it achieves is a measure of the gap in Steinbeck between the behavioral theories of the amateur biologist and the broader perspective of the artist, a gap that was to increase throughout the 1930s. He denied that the novel was anything other than a harsh scientific investigation of "man's eternal warfare with himself," saying, "I'm not interested in strike as means of raising men's wages, and I'm not interested in ranting about justice and oppression. . . . I wanted to be merely a recording consciousness, judging nothing, simply putting down the thing." Steinbeck felt that he had found in this study of the manipulations of a group of migrant workers by Communist party organizers an ideal crucible for testing the development of his group-man notions; but as soon as the material took form in a specific historical setting, Steinbeck's more complicated sympathies and prejudices altered the novel's supposed impartiality: it is not propaganda, but it clearly illustrates the problems of nonpartisanship.

Group man in *In Dubious Battle* is illustrated by a crowd of striking apple-pickers in the Torgas Valley in California. Individually, they are as far as is imaginable from the conventional image of the deserving poor: they are lazy, careless, cruel, cowardly, envious, and selfish. They refuse to cooperate voluntarily to secure even minimal sanitary arrangements for their camp. The men exploit the women sexually, and the women provoke the men to blood lust. It could never be said of these strikers, as it was of the Okies in *The Grapes of Wrath,* that they bear only the physical but not the spiritual stigmas of poverty and injustice. Yet Steinbeck refuses to indulge in such rationalizations here for the repulsive qualities of his protagonists. When these same men are unified into a group animal by the skill of Mac, the Communist organizer, the new creature is powerful, reckless of danger, savagely ferocious. It is neither more nor less decent than the individuals who compose it, but

it is vitally different in many of its attributes. There is no alternative view in the novel of American working men en masse.
The two characters who conduct the intellectual debate of the
novel over Communist tactics are in complete agreement with
this vision of group man though they differ in their responses
to it. Mac, the doctrinaire field organizer, sees the group animal
as something to be fed and goaded in the service of
Communist political ideals; his images for the group are
inevitably contemptuous animal analogies. Doc Burton, the
"dreamer, mystic, metaphysician" who gives free medical
attention to the strikers, but is himself "too God damn far left to
be a Communist," sees group man as something to be studied
and analyzed in the service of knowledge; he rejects Mac's animal images but substitutes for them images of germs and cells
that are certainly no less dehumanizing. The only denial in the
novel of the totalitarian implications of this vision of human
nature comes from the hypocritical president of the Fruit
Growers' Association, who has most to gain by it. Yet the bru-
tal detachment Steinbeck professed and aimed at in *In Dubious
Battle* is not absolute; while the group animal and its analysts
Mac and Doc Burton clearly engaged his intellectual interests, it
was not apparently a sufficient vehicle for his less impersonal
artistic sensibility. Thus the novel contains two characters, a
father and son, who remain completely outside the theoretical
scheme of the novel but who clearly have Steinbeck's sympathy. These are the Andersons, who operate a small, independent farm and a low-profit lunch wagon; they are genial,
self-reliant, and efficient men who have their livelihoods
destroyed because they side with the aims of the strikers. Since
they are so much closer than the fruit-pickers to a benevolent
image of the people, they suggest a possible evolution for
Steinbeck away from the mechanical and faceless mob—the
product of his emotional detachment—to the more heroic and
dignified people with roots in history, culture, and region who
will form the group animal in *The Grapes of Wrath.*

—Sylvia Jenkins Cook, "Steinbeck, the People, and the Party,"
Literature at the Barricades: The American Writer in the 1930s,
ed. Ralph F. Bogardus and Fred Hobson (University: University
of Alabama Press, 1982), pp. 84–86

Warren Motley on Ma Joad

[Warren Motley is a literary scholar and author of *The American Abraham: James Fenimore Cooper and the Frontier Patriarch* (1987). In this extract, Motley examines the figure of Ma Joad, finding her representative of the matriarchal values running through the novel.]

Steinbeck uses the meeting between Ma Joad and the camp manager as his principal metaphor for the matriarchal basis of governmental authority. Unlike the sheriffs and deputies Ma Joad confronts along the way, this man greets Ma Joad without condescension or hostility. With a gesture that Steinbeck has carefully prepared, the government agent squats down beside Ma Joad in the traditional posture of the tenant farmer: "He came to the fire and squatted on his hams, and the last of Ma's resistance went down" (p. 416). The emotional impact of this simple act of kindness and decency after so much insult and brutality drives home the symbolic significance of the gesture: the representative of the government meets the representative of the people's collective strength to "go on" at her own level. As the Oklahoma farmer drew strength from his independent plot of soil, this government will draw strength from the people.

Steinbeck proposes the paradox that a stronger communal government would be necessary to protect individual freedom and dignity and anticipates his readers' suspicions. Taking symbols of the red scare, political committees and barbed-wire fences, he transforms them into symbols of a democracy that protects the propertyless and allows them to participate in government. It is not the imposed patriarchal power of a totalitarian regime that protects the camp from the farmers' associations; it is not "that little guy in the office is a-stoppin' 'em," but the community's own collective strength—" 'cause we're all a-workin' together."

However, Steinbeck doubts that his America will adopt Ma Joad's matriarchal sense of community as a governing principle. He knew where power lay, and his experience forbad optimism. The camp presents only a utopian vision; it cannot provide jobs to the migrants, and the Joads are forced back to the road. As in other accounts of westward migration in our literature, Steinbeck correlates the redemption of American values with the rescue of the distressed patriarchal family. For the Joads the outlook is bleak. Ma Joad retards the family's disintegration but cannot prevent it.

At the end of the novel, Steinbeck preserves some hope, however, by insisting that Ma Joad's legacy passes on to Rose of Sharon, to Tom, and, by extension, to a future generation of Americans that might incorporate her values into democratic society. The significance of Ma Joad's bequest differs according to the sex of the two children; traditional male and female roles persist in Steinbeck's working out of matriarchal values. Rose of Sharon inherits her mother's sense of community through her womb; Tom through his mind. When Rose of Sharon offers her breast to a starving man, her smile announces her initiation into a matriarchal mystery: the capacity to nurture life. The scene confirms Ma Joad's belief that family unity can be extended to the wider community, and its shock, springing from the denial of sexuality in the meeting of man and woman, asserts Briffault's thesis that society originates not in sexual union but in maternal nurturing. As Steinbeck wrote to his editor, Rose of Sharon's offering is "a survival symbol": as a woman, she represents not the alleviation of oppression but the ability to endure it.

Tom Joad carries communal values into a more active mode. From the beginning of the novel, Tom is Ma Joad's chosen child; the core of the Joad family, as of the matriarchal clan, becomes mother and offspring rather than husband and wife. After his years in jail, Tom shares his mother's ability to live day by day on the road. Hunting down Uncle John or calming Al, Tom executes his mother's belief that the family must stay "unbroke." His eventual conversion to the labor cause is convincing in part because his new faith is firmly rooted in his mother's values. When he explains his plans to join the union—"maybe like Casy says, a fella ain't got a soul of his own, but on'y a piece of a big one," his language is not only Casy's. He follows as well his mother's more humble expression of faith—"people is goin' on." In the last days before Tom begins his mission as a labor organizer, Ma Joad claims the task of carrying food to his hiding place among the rushes. When he leaves, he receives the family's meager savings, not from his father but from Ma Joad—not when he takes over as patriarch of the family, but when he leaves the family to work for the people. Tom will tap strength that has come to the migrants by the shared experience of dispossession rather than by the individualism of his frontier heritage.

Tom's chances of staying alive, much less of relieving his people's oppression, are slim. The uncertainty of his future reflects Steinbeck's pessimism not only about the labor movement's prospects, but also about curbing the antisocial effects of individualism. However, the final image of Tom disappearing into the rushes at night has a power independent of his realistic chances of success. In the symbolic drama of the novel, his decision to follow Jim Casy and to act on the matriarchal sense of community represents the potential of the oppressed to take action—of passive endurance to become active resistance.

—Warren Motley, "From Patriarchy to Matriarchy: Ma Joad's Role in *The Grapes of Wrath*," *American Literature* 54, No. 3 (October 1982): 410–12

JOHN J. CONDER ON STEINBECK'S VIEWS OF THE HUMAN BEING'S TWO SELVES

[John J. Conder is a professor of English at Vanderbilt University and the author of *A Formula of His Own: Henry Adams's Literary Experiment* (1970). In this extract, Conder believes *The Grapes of Wrath* to be emblematic of Steinbeck's view that a human being has two selves—a group self and an individual self.]

The Grapes of Wrath is the story of the exploitation of a dispossessed group, and it is difficult not to feel that it will always engender sympathies for the dispossessed of the earth wherever and whenever they might appear. But the novel's indictment of society for what it does to individuals should have an equally enduring appeal; for here its message goes beyond the conditions of oppressed groups and addresses individuals in all strata of complex societies. The condition of individual Oklahomans in fact is an extreme representation of the condition of social man, and in the capacity of individual Oklahomans to change lies the hope for social man.

The migrants' achievement of rational freedom speaks for more than freedom for the group. It tells readers of a vital difference in kinds of freedom. Steinbeck has written, "I believe that man is a double thing—a group animal and at the same time an individual. And it occurs to me that he cannot successfully be the second until he has fulfilled the first." Only the fulfilled group self can create a successful personal self; only freedom exercised by a personal self in harmony with a group self can be significant.

This aspect of the novel's vision depends upon Steinbeck's fuller conception of an individual's two selves. One is his social self, definable by the role he plays in society and by the attitudes he has imbibed from its major institutions. The other is what is best called his species self. It contains all the biological mechanisms—his need for sexual expression, for example—that link him to other creatures in nature. And by virtue of the fact that he is thus linked to the natural world, he can feel a sense of unity with it in its inanimate as well as its animate forms. But the biological element in this self also connects him to the world of man, for it gives him an instinctive sense of identification with other members of his species, just as the members of other species have an instinctive sense of oneness with their own kind.

The species self thus has connections to nonhuman and human nature, and Steinbeck refers to the latter connection when he speaks of man as a "group animal." He views a healthy personal identity as one in which the species self in both its aspects can express itself through the social self of the individual. But society thwarts, or seeks to thwart, the expression of that self. It seeks not only to cut man off from his awareness of his connections to nonhuman nature, it seeks also to sever him from the group sense of oneness with the human species that the individual's species self possesses. Ironically, therefore, purely social man loses a sense of that unity with others which society presumably exists to promote.

The novel's social criticism rests on this view, and its emphasis on grotesques, purely social beings cut off from their connections to nature, both human and nonhuman, portrays an all-too-familiar image of modern man. In too many instances, by imposing mechanical rhythms on human nature, society creates half-men. Its repeated attempts to distort the individual's identity is emphasized by numerous dichotomies between social demands and instinct. Tom tries to comprehend the meaning of his imprisonment for killing in self-defense. Casy tries to understand the meaning of his preaching sexual abstinence when he cannot remain chaste himself. And the point is made by the basic events that set the story moving. A mechanical monster, indifferent to the maternal instincts of the Ma Joads who exercise their species selves in the interest of family solidarity, expels families from their land. The social mechanism thus tries to thwart the demands of the group aspect of the self to remain together. And the same mechanism is responsible for sowing what has become a dust bowl with cotton, rendering it permanently useless for agriculture, thus showing its indifference—nay, hostility—to the connections with nature that the species self feels.

—John J. Conder, "Steinbeck and Nature's Self: *The Grapes of Wrath*," *Naturalism in American Fiction: The Classic Phase* (Lexington: University Press of Kentucky, 1984), pp. 149–51

JOHN H. TIMMERMAN ON JIM CASY

[John H. Timmerman (b. 1945) is a professor of English at Calvin College (Grand Rapids, Michigan) and author of *Other Worlds: The Fantasy Genre* (1983), *The Dramatic Landscape of Steinbeck's Short Stories* (1990), and other works. In this extract, Timmerman studies the character of Jim Casy, believing that he is more than an analogue for Jesus Christ.]

Casy is one of the most significant characters in the novel, and through him Steinbeck establishes the broad view typified in earlier works by a character like Doc Burton. Richard Astro has argued that Doc Burton and Jim Casy are figures of Ed Ricketts, and to a certain extent both Burton and Casy represent the non-teleological view of Ricketts. Astro sees Casy as a more successful spokesman than Burton for that view in that "unlike Burton, whose vision of the whole is never converted into meaningful action, Casy knows that 'we got a job to do' and applies the principles of his perceptions to help 'the folks that don' know which way to turn.'" Casy becomes a spokesman for the movement from "I" to "we" and assumes a degree of leadership in it before he is cut down by the landowners' goons. But it is precisely that futility of leadership of a mob that stands apart from Ma Joad's enduring loving-kindness toward the family. In a sense Ma Joad is closer to Doc Burton's character than Jim Casy's; not a "party" person, she merely battles in her quiet way for human dignity. It is these quiet, almost forgotten people, like George and Lennie, that Steinbeck brings to public recognition and in whom he finds a resilient nobility.

Casy plays a significant role in the dramatic action of *The Grapes of Wrath,* however, and one can better understand Ma Joad's character by a closer examination of Casy. He has, as he says, forsaken the Holy Spirit (which he sees as being apart from man) for the human spirit. In his initial conversation with Tom, Casy provides rather unclear reasons for his conversion. He says, first, that " 'the Sperit ain't in the people no more' "; they seem forsaken, lost, and lonely. Second, " 'The Sperit ain't in me no more,' " a statement that he qualifies immediately by saying that the spirit is still strong in him but has changed from an abstract divinity to concrete action. He does not fully understand this new spirit that calls him to be a part of the people rather than apart from the people, but he recognizes that " 'I got the call to lead the people, an' no place to lead 'em.' " His effort now is to come to grips with what he calls the "human sperit." While Casy has been popularly interpreted as a Christ figure and dozens of convincing analogies are provided in the text (analogies that I would suggest Steinbeck uses to provide backdrop or "coloring" for Casy's actions), it is necessary that Casy be seen first in aesthetic terms, as a profound and moving psychological study of a man grappling with sin and human nature.

—John H. Timmerman, *John Steinbeck's Fiction: The Aesthetics of the Road Taken* (Norman: University of Oklahoma Press, 1986), pp. 113–14

LOUIS OWENS ON NATIVE AMERICANS IN *THE GRAPES OF WRATH*

[Louis Owens is a literary scholar and coauthor of *American Indian Novelists: An Annotated Critical Bibliography* (1985). In this extract, from his book on *The Grapes of Wrath,* Owen points out the importance of Native Americans in the novel: the wiping out of these peoples Indian is a symbol for the violence that underlies American settlement of the West.]

⟨. . .⟩ the presence of the American Indian in *The Grapes of Wrath* is a significant and little noted one. Given the twofold concern that runs through this novel, both for the American myth and for the kind of intuitive sense of oneness with nature expressed through Jim Casy, it is inevitable that the Indian will haunt the shadows of this American epic. ⟨. . .⟩

Most often, Steinbeck chooses to deal with flesh-and-blood "Indianness" in the form of the Mexican or Mexican-American, and in this somewhat remote, exotic form for Steinbeck the Indian need not actually be dealt with as anything more than an impulse, a shadowy presence. On the other hand, when he chose to notice the North American Indian, Steinbeck shifted ground considerably. The Indian blood enriching Mexico and Mexican-Americans serves invariably as a sign of profound, unconscious impulses, a link to the mystical. The Native American, however, tens of thousands of whom lived in Steinbeck's California during his lifetime and live there still, exists in Steinbeck's fiction purely as an index to the American Myth.

As noted above, this version of the Steinbeck Indian is introduced in *The Grapes of Wrath* when the representative sharecropper cries, "Grampa killed Indians, Pa killed snakes for the land." In this novel, the Indian is of significance only as a symbol of the destructive consciousness underlying American settlement and the westering pattern. He has mythic dimension but no further reality. When, late in the novel, the migrants gather in the evenings, Steinbeck writes: "The story tellers, gathering attention into their tales, spoke in great rhythms, spoke in great words because the tales were great, and the listeners became great through them." Here, in this romantic, epic tradition, one storyteller recalls Indian fighting on the frontier:

> They was a brave on a ridge, against the sun. . . . Spread his arms an' stood. Naked as morning, an' against the sun . . . Stood there, arms spread out; like a cross he looked. . . . An' the men—well, they raised their sights an' they felt the wind an' couldn' shoot. Maybe that Injun knowed somepin. . . . An' I laid my sights on his belly, 'cause you can't stop a Injun no other place—an'—then. Well, he jest plunked down an' rolled. An' we went up. An' he wasn' big—he'd looked so grand—up there. All tore to pieces an' little. Ever see a cock pheasant, stiff and beautiful, ever' feather drawed an' painted, an' even his eyes drawed in pretty? An' bang! You pick him up—bloody an' twisted, an' you spoiled somepin better'n you . . . you spoiled somepin in yaself, an' you can't never fix it up.

Here, naked against the sun, with arms raised in Christ-like cruciform, the Indian as symbol cuts to the heart of the idea America has of itself. In wilderness—James Fenimore Cooper's temple of nature or Henry David Thoreau's Walden—we may come closest to an unmediated spirituality, to that "part and particle of God" within the isolated self. The Indian, elemental, immersed in the fertile heart of the American wilderness garden, stands for that potential which Americans have sought for more than three centuries.

In this portrait the Indian shadows something within the American consciousness, but beyond this he has no existence and, for all the heroic grandeur of the description, he has no more human dimension than does a pheasant. The conflict between the divided self, which destroyed Danny in *Tortilla Flat,* is located implicitly within the American consciousness in

The Grapes of Wrath. In attempting to destroy the Indian, Steinbeck suggests, Americans damaged, if not destroyed that element within themselves that connected them with the earth, the intuitive self.

—Louis Owen, The Grapes of Wrath: *Trouble in the Promised Land* (Boston: Twayne, 1989), pp. 58, 60–61

WILLIAM HOWARTH ON THE ENDING OF *THE GRAPES OF WRATH*

[William Howarth (b. 1940) is the author of *The Book of Concord: Thoreau's Life as a Writer* (1982) and editor of *The John McPhee Reader* (1976). He is a professor of English at Princeton University. In this extract, Howarth defends the ending of *The Grapes of Wrath*—in which Rose of Sharon breastfeeds a starving man—against the many critics who have found it contrived or melodramatic.]

At the end of *The Grapes of Wrath,* natural and human events impel the novel to a relentless climax. Far out at sea, early winter storms rise, sweep landward, and pour drenching rain on the California mountains. Streams cascade down into river valleys, flooding the lowlands where thousands of migrant families have set up makeshift camps. Many flee, others resist—and lose their meager goods to the rising water. Having no work or wages till spring, the migrants face a hopeless situation. They begin to starve, dying from exposure and disease, but no relief arrives. The Joad family faces an added crisis, as their daughter, Rose of Sharon, suffers through hard labor and delivers a stillborn child. Water forces the clan to higher ground, where they find a boy and his starving father. The young mother lies down beside the exhausted man. She bares her breast and he feeds.

Although perplexing to generations of readers, that final tableau fulfills a design that governs Steinbeck's entire novel. His book opens with drought and ends with flood, waters that return to the earth and replenish its life. In saving a stranger,

Rose of Sharon rises from brute survival instinct into a nurturing state of grace: "She looked up and across the barn, and her lips came together and smiled mysteriously." His editor thought this ending was too enigmatic, but Steinbeck replied: "I've tried to make the reader participate in the actuality, what he takes from it will be scaled entirely on his own depth or hollowness. There are five layers in this book, a reader will find as many as he can and he won't find more than he has in himself."

In time readers have found plenty in *The Grapes of Wrath,* calling it a pack of lies, an American epic, an act of art wrapped in propaganda. This multeity of response bathed the author in ironies. His book denounced capitalism but rang up towering sales; its fame brought him wealth and power yet ruined him for greater work. "There is a failure here that topples all our success," he wrote of the Depression, words that could also eulogize his own career. Why did this comet rise in his thirty-seventh summer, and what were its literary origins? Critics have tended to cite the modernist traditions of realism or symbolism, either aligning Steinbeck with social ideology—Farrell, Herbst, Wright—or with the cultural esthetics of Dos Passos and Faulkner. Both traditions regard creativity as a lonely, heroic struggle, fought by artists for the sake of their people. Robert DeMott speaks for this consensus in calling *The Grapes of Wrath* "a private tragedy," in which the writer sacrificed "the unique qualities . . . that made his art exemplary" (W*xlvi*) to create a broad social novel.

That vision of martyred demise may explain Steinbeck's later career, but it refutes the meaning of his greatest triumph. The novel's final scene is not a rite of sacrifice but fulfillment, as individual striving gives way to shared alliance. Two persons become one, not through sex or even love, but through their selfless flow into a broader stream, the rising water of human endurance. The novel repeats this idea in many contexts, most notably through Jim Casy, a prophet who fuses the socialist vision of class struggle with a sacramental longing for universal communion: "But when they're all workin' together, not one fella for another fella, but one fella kind of harnessed to the whole shebang—that's right, that's holy." If these ideas hark back to Depression-era politics, they also anticipate a world that has yet to come, tied in bonds of ecological affinity.

—William Howarth, "The Mother of Literature: Journalism and *The Grapes of Wrath*," *New Essays on* The Grapes of Wrath, ed. David Wyatt (Cambridge: University of Cambridge Press, 1990), pp. 71–73

❖

Susan Shillinglaw on Corporate Farmers' Attacks on *The Grapes of Wrath*

[Susan Shillinglaw is a professor of English at San Jose State University and the author of several articles on Steinbeck. In this extract, Shillinglaw examines the responses of a variety of corporate farmers to Steinbeck's novel, showing that their vision of a prosperous California was arrived at through a willful avoidance of the plight of the migrant workers.]

Four months after publication of *The Grapes of Wrath,* John Steinbeck responded sharply to mounting criticism of his book: "I know what I was talking about," he told a *Los Angeles Times* reporter. "I lived, off and on, with those Okies for the last three years. Anyone who tries to refute me will just become ridiculous." His angry retort is largely on target—but the opposition was in earnest and had been even before his novel was published.

In 1938 corporate farmers in California responded forcefully to the consequences of continued migration: the twin threats of unions and a liberal migrant vote. Beginning early that year a statewide publicity campaign to discredit the "migrant menace" had been mounted by the Associated Farmers and the newly formed CCA, or California Citizens Association, a group with the broad support of banks, oil companies, agricultural land companies, businesses, and public utilities. Well-funded and well-placed, the CCA and the Associated Farmers produced scores of articles meant to discourage further migration, to encourage Dust Bowlers already in California to return to their home states, and to convince the federal government that California's migrant problem was a federal, not a state, responsibility. These articles vigorously defended farmers' wage scales and housing standards. They complained about the state's generous relief, which, at almost twice that of Oklahoma and Arkansas, had "encouraged" migration. And they often maligned the state's newest residents. "The whole design of modern life," noted an article in the *San Francisco Examiner* entitled "The Truth About California," "has stimulated their hunger for change and adventure, fun and frippery. Give them a relief check and they'll head straight for a beauty shop and a movie." The publication of Steinbeck's novel in March 1939—followed shortly thereafter by Carey McWilliams's carefully documented *Factories in the Fields*—simply gave the outraged elite a new focus for their attack.

The campaign took on a new intensity. Editorials and pamphlets, many underwritten by the Associated Farmers, claimed to expose Steinbeck's "prejudice, exaggeration, and oversimplification," the thesis of one tract, or to discredit the "Termites Steinbeck and McWilliams," the title of another. Of greater impact, however, were the more sustained efforts to counter what were perceived as Steinbeck's factual inaccuracies. I shall examine four of the most important respondents. Two who defended California agriculture were highly respected professional writers: Ruth Comfort Mitchell, the author of *Of Human Kindness,* and Frank J. Taylor, a free-lance journalist who covered California business, farming, and recreation for the state and national press. And two were highly successful retired farmers, to use the word loosely: Marshall V. Hartranft, the Los Angeles fruit grower and real estate developer who wrote *Grapes of Gladness: California's Refreshing and Inspiring Answer to John Steinbeck's* Grapes of Wrath, and Sue Sanders, touted as the "friend of the migrant," who wrote and published a tract called "The Real Causes of Our Migrant Problem." Since each contributed to what can only be called a hysterical campaign against the migrant presence and Steinbeck himself, it is difficult not to cast them as villains. What must be recognized, however, is that each with great sincerity and, to a large extent, accuracy, described another California—a brawny, confident state that bustled with entrepreneurial zeal. Each defended California against Steinbeck's charges largely by ignoring much of the agony and cruelty he chronicled. Each sought an answer to the "migrant question" without fully comprehending—or perhaps, more significantly, empathizing with—the "problem," the migrants' plight. To understand each writer's perspective is to appreciate better the intensity of the political clashes of the 1930s, a period when, as liberal activist Richard Criley observed, "Social issues were so sharp and so clear . . . we were pulled to take a position because things were so acute, so terrifying in the need to change." These interpreters of the California scene resisted change.

—Susan Shillinglaw, "California Answers *The Grapes of Wrath*," *John Steinbeck: The Years of Greatness 1936–1939,* ed. Tetsamuro Hayashi (Tuscaloosa: University of Alabama Press, 1993), pp. 145–47

WARREN FRENCH ON INDIVIDUAL AND SOCIETY IN *THE GRAPES OF WRATH*

[Warren French (b. 1922) is a professor of English at Indiana University–Purdue University at Indianapolis and a prolific literary scholar. Among his books are *John Steinbeck* (1961; rev. 1975), *J. D. Salinger* (1963; rev. 1976), *The Social Novel at the End of an Era* (1966), and *Jack Kerouac* (1986). In this extract from his recent study of Steinbeck, French shows how Steinbeck transformed the story of a single family, the Joads, into a broader account of problems affecting society at large.]

Trying to avoid the problem that *The Grapes of Wrath* would be interpreted as the unique account of one family's troubled pilgrimage, Steinbeck paired the chapters narrating the history of the Joads with others that show the broader significance of the things that happen to them.

Although nowhere in the novel (or in his later published journal of its writing) does the author identify the method he is using, he does carefully explain—as Peter Lisca pointed out in *The Wide World of John Steinbeck*—a conscious intention behind his procedure in his preface to the voice-over narrative from his film *The Forgotten Village* (1941), illustrated with stills from the film. Commenting on the problems he faced in creating this account of the introduction of scientific medicine into a remote, superstition-ridden Mexican village, Steinbeck explained, "A great many documentary films have used the generalized method, that is, the showing of a condition or an event as it affects a group of people. . . . In *The Forgotten Village* we reversed the usual process. Our story centered on one family in one small village. We wished our audience to know this family very well, and incidentally to like it, as we did. Then, from association with this little personalized group, the larger conclusion concerning the racial group can be drawn with something like participation." In *The Grapes of Wrath* Steinbeck had not taken a chance on one method or the other; he had used both to help get his points across. The Joad story, like *The Forgotten Village,* focuses on one family, while the "generalized method" is used in the interchapters. By presenting the situations that distressed him through the history of one family, he obliged readers to visualize the affected individuals and denied escapists the distancing consolation of the sociology textbooks' treatment of problem groups in numbers too large to be easily comprehended.

On the other hand, by using the generalized method he refuted any charges that the history of the Joads was unique and solely fictional. In the device of the interchapter he found exactly the technique he needed to make his "big" novel simultaneously a general tract and an intensely personal history of the frightening situation of a culture in transition.

This last description, however, limits the novel too much to a depiction of a particular time and place. The novel is more than a period piece about a troubled past era; it is also an allegory, applicable wherever prejudice and a haughty sense of self-importance inhibit cooperation.

In a letter to Pascal Covici in January 1939, defending the final scene of the novel and refusing to change it, Steinbeck stressed that there are "five layers in this book," "a reader will find as many as he can," and "what he takes from it will be scaled entirely on his own depth or hollowness." Nothing so far published provides any specific indication of his conception of these five layers, but speculation might well begin with the most famous explanation of "levels of meaning" in literature, which comes from St. Thomas Aquinas but is most usefully presented by Dante, who drew on Aquinas in *Convivio:*

> Exposition must be *literal* and *allegorical.* And for the understanding of this you should know that writings can be understood and must be explained, for the most part, in four senses. One is called *literal;* and this is the one which extends not beyond the letter itself. The next is called *allegorical;* and this is the one which is hidden beneath the cloak of these fables. . . . The third sense is called *moral;* and this is the one which readers must ever diligently observe in writings, for their own profit and for that of their pupils. . . . The fourth sense is called *anagogical* or supersensual; and this is when we expound spiritually a writing which, even in the letter, through the very things exprest expresseth things concerning eternal glory.

In a famous letter to his friend Can Grande della Scala, Dante, explaining his own *Divine Comedy,* applied these concepts to the biblical story of the Exodus from Egypt, which many critics argue influenced *The Grapes of Wrath:* "If we look to the *letter* alone, we are told of the going forth of the children from Egypt in the time of Moses; if we look at the *allegory,* we are told of our future redemption through Christ; if we consider the *moral* sense, we are told of the conversion of the soul from the grief and misery of sin to the state of grace; if we consider the *anagogical,* we are told of the going forth of the blessed soul from the servitude of corruption to the freedom of eternal glory."

—Warren French, *John Steinbeck's Fiction Revisited* (New York: Twayne, 1994), pp. 81–83

❧

Books by
John Steinbeck

Cup of Gold: A Life of Henry Morgan, Buccaneer, with Occasional Reference to History. 1929.

The Pastures of Heaven. 1932.

To a God Unknown. 1933.

Tortilla Flat. 1935.

In Dubious Battle. 1936.

Saint Katy the Virgin. 1936.

Nothing So Monstrous. 1936.

Of Mice and Men. 1937.

Of Mice and Men (drama). 1937.

The Red Pony. 1937.

The Long Valley. 1938.

Their Blood Is Strong. 1938.

The Grapes of Wrath. 1939.

John Steinbeck Replies. 1940.

The Forgotten Village. 1941.

Sea of Cortez: A Leisurely Journal of Travel and Research (with Edward F. Ricketts). 1941.

Bombs Away: The Story of a Bomber Team. 1942.

The Moon Is Down. 1942.

The Moon Is Down (drama). 1943.

The Steinbeck Pocket Book. Ed. Pascal Covici. 1943.

How Edith McGillcuddy Met R L S. 1943.

Cannery Row. 1945.

The Portable Steinbeck. Ed. Pascal Covici. 1946.

The Pearl. 1947.

Vanderbilt Clinic. 1947.

The Wayward Bus. 1947.

The First Watch. 1947.

A Russian Journal. 1948.

The Steinbeck Omnibus. 1950.

Burning Bright: A Play in Story Form. 1950.

Burning Bright (drama). 1951.

Viva Zapata! 1951, 1991 (as *Zapata*).

The Log from the Sea of Cortez. 1951.

East of Eden. 1952.

Short Novels. 1953.

Sweet Thursday. 1954.

Positano. 1954.

The Short Reign of Pippin IV: A Fabrication. 1957.

The Chrysanthemums. 1957.

Once There Was a War. 1958.

The Winter of Our Discontent. 1961.

Travels with Charley in Search of America. 1962.

Speech Accepting the Nobel Prize for Literature. c. 1962.

A Letter from John Steinbeck. 1964.

Letters to Alicia. 1965.

America and Americans. 1966.

The Journal of a Novel: The East of Eden *Letters.* 1969.

John Steinbeck: His Language. 1970.

Steinbeck: A Life in Letters. Ed. Elaine Steinbeck and Robert Wallsten. 1975.

The Acts of King Arthur and His Noble Knights, from the Winchester Manuscripts of Malory and Other Sources. 1976.

The Collected Poems of Amnesia Glasscock. 1976.

Letters to Elizabeth: A Selection of Letters from John Steinbeck to Elizabeth Otis. Ed. Florian J. Shasky and Susan F. Riggs. 1978.

Flight. 1979.

A Letter of Inspiration. 1980.

Selected Essays. Ed. Kiyoshi Nakayama and Hidekazu Hirose. 1981.

Your Only Weapon Is Your Work: A Letter by John Steinbeck to Dennis Murphy. 1985.

Uncollected Stories. Ed. Kiyoshi Nakayama. 1986.

Always Something to Do in Salinas. 1986.

John Steinbeck on Writing. Ed. Tetsumaro Hayashi. 1988.

Working Days: The Journals of The Grapes of Wrath *1938–1941.* Ed. Robert DeMott. 1989.

"Their Blood Is Strong." 1989.

Breakfast: A Short Story. 1990.

Novels and Stories 1932–1937. 1994.

Works about John Steinbeck and *The Grapes of Wrath*

Astro, Richard. *John Steinbeck and Edward F. Ricketts: The Shaping of a Novelist.* Minneapolis: University of Minnesota Press, 1973.

Benson, Jackson J. " 'To Tom, Who Lived It': John Steinbeck and the Man from Weedpatch." *Journal of Modern Literature* 5 (1976): 151–94.

———. *The True Adventures of John Steinbeck, Writer: A Biography.* New York: Viking Press, 1983.

Bloom, Harold, ed. *John Steinbeck.* New York: Chelsea House, 1987.

———, ed. *John Steinbeck's* The Grapes of Wrath. New York: Chelsea House, 1988.

Bluefarb, Sam. "The Joads: Flight into the Social Soul." In Bluefarb's *The Escape Motif in the American Novel: Mark Twain to Richard Wright.* Columbus: Ohio State University Press, 1972, pp. 94–112.

Bowron, Bernard. "*The Grapes of Wrath:* A 'Wagons West' Romance." *Colorado Quarterly* 3, No. 1 (Summer 1954): 84–91.

Brasch, James D. "*The Grapes of Wrath* and Old Testament Skepticism." *San Jose Studies* 3, No. 2 (1977): 16–27.

Browning, Chris. "Grapes Symbolism in *The Grapes of Wrath.*" *Discourse* 11 (1968): 129–40.

Carlson, Eric W. "Symbolism in *The Grapes of Wrath.*" *College English* 19 (1957–58): 172–75.

Cassuto, David. "Turning Wine into Water: Water as Privileged Signifier in *The Grapes of Wrath.*" *Papers on Language and Literature* 29 (1993): 67–95.

Cox, Martha Heasley. "The Conclusion of *The Grapes of Wrath:* Steinbeck's Concept and Execution." *San Jose Studies* 1, No. 3 (1975): 73–81.

Crockett, H. Kelly. "The Bible and *The Grapes of Wrath.*" *College English* 24 (1962–63): 193–99.

Davis, Robert Con, ed. *Twentieth-Century Interpretations of* The Grapes of Wrath: *A Collection of Critical Essays.* Englewood Cliffs, NJ: Prentice-Hall, 1982.

DeMott, Robert. " 'Working Days and Hours': Steinbeck's Writing of *The Grapes of Wrath.*" *Studies in American Fiction* 18 (1990): 3–15.

Ditsky, John, ed. *Critical Essays on* The Grapes of Wrath. Boston: G. K. Hall, 1989.

———. "*The Grapes of Wrath:* A Reconsideration." *Southern Humanities Review* 13 (1979): 215–20.

Donohue, Agnes M., ed. *A Casebook on* The Grapes of Wrath. New York: Crowell, 1968.

Eisinger, Chester E. "Jeffersonian Agrarianism in *The Grapes of Wrath.*" *University of Kansas City Review* 14 (1947): 149–54.

Fossey, W. Richard. "The End of the Western Dream: *The Grapes of Wrath* and Oklahoma." *Cimarron Review* 22 (1973): 25–34.

French, Warren. *A Companion to* The Grapes of Wrath. New York: Viking, 1963 (rev. ed. 1989).

———. *John Steinbeck.* New York: Twayne, 1961 (rev. ed. 1975).

Garcia, Reloy. "The Rocky Road to Eldorado: The Journey Motif in John Steinbeck's *The Grapes of Wrath.*" *Steinbeck Quarterly* 14 (1981): 83–93.

———. *Steinbeck and D. H. Lawrence: Fictive Voices and the Ethical Imperative.* Muncie, IN: John Steinbeck Society of America, 1972.

Gladstein, Mimi Reisel. *The Indestructible Woman in Faulkner, Hemingway, and Steinbeck.* Ann Arbor, MI: UMI Research Press, 1986.

Gray, James. *John Steinbeck.* Minneapolis: University of Minnesota Press, 1971.

Griffin, Robert J., and William A. Freedman. "Machines and Animals: Pervasive Motifs in *The Grapes of Wrath*." *Journal of English and Germanic Philology* 62 (1963): 569–80.

Hayashi, Tetsumaro, ed. The Grapes of Wrath: *Essays in Criticism*. Muncie, IN: Steinbeck Research Institute, 1990.

———, ed. *Steinbeck's Women: Essays in Criticism*. Muncie, IN: John Steinbeck Society of America, 1979.

Hunter, J. Paul. "Steinbeck's Wine of Affirmation in *The Grapes of Wrath*." In *Essays in Modern American Literature*, ed. Richard E. Langford. DeLand, FL: Stetson University Press, 1963, pp. 76–89.

Hyman, Stanley Edgar. "Some Notes on John Steinbeck." *Antioch Review* 2 (1942): 185–200.

Jones, Lawrence William. *John Steinbeck as Fabulist*. Ed. Marston LaFrance. Muncie, IN: John Steinbeck Society of America, 1973.

Kiernan, Thomas. *The Intricate Music: A Biography of John Steinbeck*. Boston: Little, Brown, 1979.

Lieber, Todd M. "Talismanic Patterns in the Novels of John Steinbeck." *American Literature* 44 (1972): 262–75.

Lisca, Peter. "*The Grapes of Wrath* as Fiction." *PMLA* 72 (1957): 296–309.

———. *John Steinbeck: Nature and Myth*. New York: Crowell, 1978.

———. *The Wide World of John Steinbeck*. New Brunswick, NJ: Rutgers University Press, 1958.

McCarthy, Paul. "House and Shelter as Symbol in *The Grapes of Wrath*." *South Dakota Review* 5, No. 4 (1967–68): 48–67.

———. *John Steinbeck*. New York: Ungar, 1980.

Marks, Lester Jay. *Thematic Design in the Novels of John Steinbeck*. The Hague: Mouton, 1969.

Modern Fiction Studies 11, No. 1 (Spring 1965). Special John Steinbeck issue.

Mullen, Patrick B. "American Folklife and *The Grapes of Wrath*." *Journal of American Culture* 1, No. 4 (Winter 1978): 742–53.

Noble, Donald R., ed. *The Steinbeck Question: New Essays in Criticism.* Troy, NY: Whitston, 1993.

Owen, Louis. *John Steinbeck's Re-Vision of America.* Athens: University of Georgia Press, 1985.

Parini, Jay. *John Steinbeck: A Biography.* London: Heinemann, 1994.

Pizer, Donald. "John Steinbeck: *The Grapes of Wrath.*" In Pizer's *Twentieth-Century American Literary Naturalism: An Interpretation.* Carbondale: Southern Illinois University Press, 1982.

Pollock, Theodore. "On the Ending of *The Grapes of Wrath.*" *Modern Fiction Studies* 4 (1958): 177–78.

Pratt, John Clark. *John Steinbeck: A Critical Essay.* Grand Rapids, MI: William B. Eerdmans, 1970.

Rombold, Tamara. "Biblical Inversion in *The Grapes of Wrath.*" *College Literature* 14 (1987): 146–66.

St. Pierre, Brian. *John Steinbeck: The California Years.* San Francisco: Chronicle Books, 1983.

Shockley, Martin Staples. "The Reception of *The Grapes of Wrath* in Oklahoma." *American Literature* 15 (1943–44): 351–61.

Simmonds, Roy S. *Steinbeck's Literary Achievements.* Muncie, IN: John Steinbeck Society of America, 1976.

Slade, Leonard A., Jr. "The Use of Biblical Allusions in *The Grapes of Wrath.*" *CLA Journal* 11 (1968): 241–47.

Taylor, Walter Fuller. "*The Grapes of Wrath* Reconsidered." *Mississippi Quarterly* 12 (1959): 136–44.

Tedlock, E. W., Jr., and C. V. Wicker, ed. *Steinbeck and His Critics: A Record of Twenty-five Years.* Albuquerque: University of New Mexico Press, 1965.

Timmerman, John H. "The Squatter's Circle in *The Grapes of Wrath.*" *Studies in American Fiction* 17 (1989): 203–11.

Zollman, Sol. "John Steinbeck's Political Outlook in *The Grapes of Wrath.*" *Literature and Ideology* 13 (1972): 9–20.

Index of Themes and Ideas

BURTON, DOC (*In Dubious Battle*), compared to Jim Casy, 54; and group behavior in *The Grapes of Wrath*, 48

CASY, JIM, and Emersonian transcendentalism, 30–33, 37–38, 41, 55, 58; as Jesus Christ, 38, 39–42, 53, 54; and his role in the novel, 13, 14, 15, 17, 18, 20, 22, 25, 28, 43, 50, 51, 53–55

COMMUNITY, DIFFERENT FORMS OF, as theme, 18, 22, 46–48

GRAPES OF WRATH, THE: allegory in, 42–44, 63; corporate farmers' attacks on, 59–61; artificiality of dialogue, 29–30; ending of, 57–59; portrayal of the individual and society in, 61–63; Native Americans in, 55–57; as propaganda, 27–29, 47, 58; religious symbolism of, 39–42

GRAVES, MULEY, and his role in the novel, 13, 25

IN DUBIOUS BATTLE, compared with *The Grapes of Wrath,* 47–48

JOAD, AL, and his role in the novel, 14, 16, 20, 21, 22, 24

JOAD, GRAMPA, and his role in the novel, 14, 15, 22, 25, 28, 34, 44, 45, 56

JOAD, GRANMA, and her role in the novel, 14, 17, 25, 28, 45

JOAD, (UNCLE) JOHN, and his role in the novel, 13, 21–24, 40, 41, 43

JOAD, MA: and matriarchal values, 49–51; and her role in the novel, 14, 15, 17, 18, 20–24, 28, 32, 33, 34, 37, 38, 40, 51, 53, 54

JOAD, NOAH, and his role in the novel, 14, 17, 22, 34

JOAD, PA (Tom Joad, Sr.), and his role in the novel, 14, 21–24, 40, 51, 56

JOAD, ROSE OF SHARON, and her role in the novel, 14, 16, 17, 18, 20, 22–24, 25, 34, 37, 40, 43, 50, 57, 58

JOAD, RUTHIE, and her role in the novel, 14, 19, 21, 22, 25, 43

JOAD, TOM, and his role in the novel, 12–22, 24, 25, 31, 32, 37–41, 43, 45, 50, 51, 53

JOAD, WINFIELD, and his role in the novel, 14, 20, 21, 22, 25, 43

KNOWLES, FLOYD, and his role in the novel, 17, 18, 25–26

MAC (*In Dubious Battle*), and group behavior in *The Grapes of Wrath*, 47–48

OF MICE AND MEN, comparisons with *The Grapes of Wrath*, 34

RAWLEY, JIM, 18, 26

RIVERS, CONNIE, and his role in the novel, 14, 16, 18, 22, 24–25, 34, 40

RUGGED INDIVIDUALISM, as theme, 18, 19

SENTIMENTALISM, 16, 33–34, 39

STEINBECK, JOHN: experiences with agricultural workers, 8–9, 35–37; interest in group behavior, 46–48, 51–53; letters of, 35–37, 62; life of, 8–11; ignorance of Okies, 44–46; views on the group self and the individual self, 51–53

STOICISM, as a theme, 18

SUFFERING, as a theme, 37, 39

THOMAS, MR., and his role in the novel, 19, 26

WAINWRIGHT, AGGIE, and her role in the novel, 21, 22, 24

WILSON, IVY, and his role in the novel, 15, 16, 17, 25

WILSON, SAIRY, and her role in the novel, 15, 16, 17, 25